Celebration Press Reading
Good Habits Great Readers™

Celebration Press Reading
Good Habits Great Readers™
Writing

The balanced-literacy solution for K–5

Celebration Press Reading Good Habits Great Readers™ now includes *Good Habits Great Readers*™ *Writing*—a companion program to meet your classroom writing needs.

Connected seamlessly, these two unique programs offer you a balanced, all-in-one solution for reading and writing instruction to reduce preparation time and maximize student learning.

See reverse for details

PEARSON

Good Habits, Great Readers

Building the Literacy Community

Nancy Frey
San Diego State University

Douglas Fisher
San Diego State University

Adam Berkin

Allyn & Bacon
is an imprint of

Boston New York San Francisco
Mexico City Montreal Toronto London Madrid Munich Paris
Hong Kong Singapore Tokyo Cape Town Sydney

Vice President and Executive Publisher: Jeffrey W. Johnston
Senior Editor: Linda Ashe Bishop
Senior Development Editor: Hope Madden
Senior Project Manager: Mary M. Irvin
Editorial Assistant: Demetrius Hall
Senior Art Director: Diane C. Lorenzo
Cover Designer: Jeff Vanik
Cover Image: Jupiter Images
Production Manager: Matt Ottenweller
Director of Marketing: David Gesell
Marketing Manager: Darcy Betts Prybella
Marketing Coordinator: Brian Mounts

For related titles and support materials, visit our online catalog at www.pearsonhighered.com

---

Library of Congress Cataloging-in-Publication Data

Frey, Nancy
Good habits, great readers: building the literacy community/Nancy Frey, Douglas Fisher, Adam Berkin.
p. cm.
Includes bibliographical references and index.
ISBN-13: 978-0-13-159717-4
1. Reading. 2. Children–Books and reading. I. Fisher, Douglas. II. Berkin, Adam. III. Title.
LB1050.F685 2009
428.4071—dc22 2008003350

Printed in the United States of America

10 9 8 7 6 5 4 3 2 1 [STO] 12 11 10 09 08

Allyn & Bacon
is an imprint of

ACKNOWLEDGMENTS

We would like to thank the teachers, colleagues, and friends who made this text possible. Thank you Aida Allen, Maureen Begley, Linda Bishop, Helen Comba, Linda Dorf, Rita Elwardi, Cora Five, Hope Madden, Christine Fleming McIsaac, Christine Johnson, Adria Klein, Diane Lapp, Bill Laraway, Lee Mongrue, Kelly Moore, Wendy Murray, Pam Musick, Joan Novelli, Tracey Randinelli, Alex Rivas-Smith, Sheryl Segal, Sheri Sevenbergen, Elizabeth Soriano, Ellen Ungaro, and Doug Williams.

We are also indebted to the reviewers who offered their thoughtful comments as this work progressed. Joetta Beaver; Beth Cavanaugh, Poudre School District; Dawn Downes, University of Delaware; Jill Flodstrom, University of Illinois; Barbara Pettegrew, Otterbein College; Laura Robb; and Gail Tompkins, California State University. Their feedback made this a better book, and we thank them.

BRIEF CONTENTS

CONTENTS

INTRODUCTION

You may be wondering whether the book you are holding in your hands is different from the many others you've read on reading comprehension. You're probably asking yourself, "What's new?" or "Can I really use this?" Before we answer those questions, let us tell you why we wrote this book. Across the country, teachers are being asked to do more, often with less. As teachers, we feel the pressure to perform, to make adequate yearly progress, and to intervene with every student while faithfully implementing a reading program.

And all of this comes at a time when we've broken reading down into bits and parts and understand more about this invisible process than ever before. At this point in our collective history, there really is the potential for all students to master this symbol system. Unfortunately, it's also a time in which teachers hear only about strategy after strategy, but not about ways to integrate these strategies and skills into habits that students can use year after year.

Yes, we think about all of this, but that wasn't enough to compel us to write. Something else pushed us over the proverbial bridge. It has become more popular of late to suggest that students don't need reading comprehension strategy instruction. Some authors have said that all the strategy instruction has served to impede true comprehension. This just didn't fit with our experience. Our research and experience have shown us that readers need, and benefit from, explicit instruction in how to activate strategies to support their understanding of text. But we also realized that isolated strategy instruction isn't getting us where we need to go. Though we learned a lot from *Mosaic of Thought* and *Strategies that Work*, we know that it takes more to master reading than learning seven comprehension strategies. In order for students to move beyond self-consciously, and sometimes artificially, implementing a strategy, we have to teach for habits. And we realized that we knew something about that. We were obliged to write about our experiences in going from good reading teachers to great reading teachers; from building good readers to building great readers; from strategies to habits.

In doing so, we clarified our thinking and learned a lot. This book is the outcome of all of our experiences in teaching hundreds of children to read and write. It's also our plea to make school reading more like reading in the real word. Therefore, in this book you will find examples of adult reading that illustrate how a school-based reading comprehension strategy is realized as the habit of an independent and self-sustaining reader. After all, our goal is to develop lifelong readers who engage with texts because they want to, not because they must.

Along the way, we found a wonderful poem that we'd like to share with you. We think you'll agree that Francisco Gomes de Matos captured the wonders of reading and what reading can do for the world. With this in mind, we hope that this is the book for you, that it is worth your time, and that it provides you with ideas you can use tomorrow and for the years to come. We hope this book creates a conversation about teaching reading that extends beyond the current obsession with strategies and focuses attention on habits—habits that readers need to engage with the world around them.

Reading is . . . *by Francisco Gomes de Matos*

READING is forming
informing
reforming
transforming

READING is ascending
descending
transcending

READING is lightening
delighting
enlightening

READING is covering
recovering
discovering

READING is conceiving
receiving
perceiving

READING is mind-using
mind-musing
mind-amusing
mind-infusing

Source: Reading Today (June/July 2007), International Reading Association. Used with permission.

CHAPTER 1

Going From Good to Great

Here's an easy question: What's your definition of a great reader? To answer this question, it might help to picture a student, current or past, that you consider a great reader. Think. When you met with this student's parents or wrote his or her report card, how did you describe this student as a reader? Notice that we've intentionally used the word "great" here, not "strategic," "proficient," or "good." Before you keep reading, jot down your definition, or at least some characteristics of a great reader, right here on a margin. Throughout this book, we are going to ask you to revisit this definition.

Before we dive into reading research, let's explore the difference between good and great. Jim Collins (2001), a business and organization guru, asks, "Can a good company become a great company and if so, how?" To answer this question, he reviewed the performance of 1,435 companies. His answer: Going from good to great doesn't require access to the latest and fastest technology, an innovative or well-known leader, standardized management procedures, or even a fine-tuned business plan. Collins profiles 11 companies from his original list of 1,435 that made substantial improvements over time. What was unique about these truly great companies was the creation of a culture that rigorously identified and encouraged people to think and act.

We think Collins identified an essential truth, not about business, but about human development. Imagine a classroom, and even a school, where everyone from student to teacher was encouraged *to think and to act.* Go back to your definition of a great reader; did it include anything about "thinking" and "acting"? Perhaps it didn't include these specific words, but chances are it did include the sense that a great reader is independent and self-motivated, a great reader thinks about text and "acts" when text doesn't make sense and is influenced by the text to act.

Precision in Our Teaching

We believe what we *need* to go from good to great in our classrooms, and in our schools, is to achieve more precision in our teaching. Fullan, Hill, and Crévola (2006) define precision as "a system that matches the short-term effects of direct instruction while building the conditions for longer-term effects" (p. 12). Teaching with precision requires that we:

- Assess the literacy development of our students,
- Understand both the short- and long-term purposes of our instruction, and
- Facilitate students' literacy habits, and plan for needs-based instructional interventions.

What we *don't need* is a greater emphasis on scripted programs that remove thinking from the classroom. That's not to say that we don't need access to quality instructional materials—we do. The difference between the prescription of scripted programs that focus on short-term purposes and a precision approach that teaches both the skills needed and their application is an important distinction, and one we hope to make throughout this book. In other words, we will explore ways to make your teaching more precise. For now, let's return to our original question: What makes a great reader? Let's see what we can learn from the history of reading instruction.

Getty Images, Inc.-Stockbyte

A Brief History of Literacy Instruction

For decades, reading teachers and reading researchers have disagreed about the best way to create literate individuals. In *Changing our Minds: Negotiating English and Literacy*, Miles Myers (1996) explains how the very definition of literacy has evolved over the years. It wasn't too long ago that being able to sign your name meant you were literate. As literacy education in our society progressed, people had to be able to copy long passages of documents in order to take them westward. By the latter half of the 19th century, society began to value recitational literacy. Recitational literacy placed a high value on your ability to recite. Remember those scenes of the one-room schoolhouse on *Little House on the Prairie* when Laura and her classmates had to recite long poems and historical documents like the Declaration of Independence from memory? From there, the hallmark of 20th century education became analytic literacy. The emphasis was on finding the "right" answer—"What is the role of religion in *Beowulf*?" The study guide industry made millions providing the answers to those analytical literacy questions.

In the 21st century, we've embraced critical literacy, an approach that suggests that readers should question the text, wonder about the author's message, and determine whose story *isn't* being told. Myers reminds us that it doesn't mean that those earlier permutations of literacy have lost their importance. Instead, each of those earlier definitions function as an entry point to the next. Likewise, our definition of what constitutes an effective reader continues to evolve as the literacy demands of our society grow.

As the definition of literacy evolved, so did our methods of teaching literacy. In an effort to improve achievement in the 21st century, the government has focused attention on the components of reading. At the request of the U.S. Congress, the National Reading Panel produced a report to provide guidance to teachers, administrators, and researchers on effective reading instruction (National Institute of Child Health and Human Development, 2000a). They clustered their findings into areas of reading process, often called the five pillars of reading: phonics, phonemics awareness, fluency, vocabulary, and comprehension.

Students need explicit and guided instruction in each of these areas to become proficient readers. Our focus for this book, however, is on comprehension. Of course, decoding words, knowing the word's meaning, and reading fast enough to make sense of the text are critical to comprehension. Those are givens. Our interest, however, focuses on comprehension strategy instruction. The comprehension subgroup of the National Reading Panel analyzed 481 studies and described comprehension instruction in three dimensions.

1. The development of an awareness and understanding of the reader's own cognitive processes that are amenable to instruction and learning.
2. A teacher guiding the reader or modeling for the reader the actions that the reader can take to enhance comprehension processes used during reading.
3. The reader practicing those strategies with the teacher assisting until the reader achieves a gradual internalization and independent mastery of those processes. (National Institute of Child Health and Human Development, 2000b, p. 3)

In other words, effective comprehension instruction involves causing students to notice their understandings through modeled and guided instruction with a teacher who scaffolds toward increasing independence.

But this definition leaves us still asking about what good and great readers do when they read and if there are behaviors we can teach our students. A number of people and organizations have described good readers.

- Gay Su Pinnell (n.d.) observes, "Good readers do not simply 'practice' reading; they have a range of purposes and objectives."
- The Texas Education Agency (2002) suggests "good readers actively and consciously coordinate these skills and strategies before, during and after reading a text."
- The fourth-grade students in Jill Johnson's (2005) study listed 72 things good readers do, including "read a lot," "read with expression," and "make no mistakes."

We are awash with information about the strategies good readers use while reading (e.g., Harvey & Goudvis, 2007; Keene & Zimmerman, 1997; Pressley, 2000). These strategies include inferencing, making connections, visualizing, determining importance, synthesizing, questioning, and using text structures.

A Focus on Habits

All of this research helps us identify the characteristics of good readers and the teaching methods necessary to produce good readers. But for us this bar is too low; we don't want good, we want great! We have great ambitions and goals for our teaching. We want instruction that will close the achievement gap. We want to ensure that all students reach high levels of literacy achievement. To return to Jim Collins, we want to go from good to great. Teaching our students all the skills and strategies will make them good; teaching them all the skills and strategies + HABITS will make them GREAT!

Habits represent the long-term conditions of learning associated with a precision approach to teaching. It means that over time, students learn how to activate strategies so smoothly that they become skills that no longer need to be mediated consciously. Here's a case in point.

Zack is a reasonably good reader. He's had a lot of strategy instruction and can define each and every one of the strategies we've listed above. He knows the difference between inferencing and predicting. He regularly writes down questions about his reading. And he dutifully summarizes each reading selection in his journal. As we've said, he's a reasonably good reader. But he's not a great reader. Zack doesn't think and act like a reader. He doesn't choose to read on his own and he doesn't integrate these strategies into habits. He knows how to read and does so when asked. He engages in each strategy that has been taught to him, when it is required as an activity or assignment. For some people that might be good enough. We know that there are a number of struggling readers and that their teachers would love to see them engage in these behaviors.

Hope Madden/Merrill

For us, it's not enough. The bar is just too low. Zack needs to develop habits, and we need to push him to move from good (enough) to great. As such, our goal for Zack should be that he become a skilled reader, not simply a strategic reader. For us, a skilled reader is a great reader. Let's explore this difference in greater depth.

Strategic or Skilled Readers?

Students use many strategies and skills when learning to read. Experts differentiate between what is a strategy and what is a skill in different ways. Paris, Wasik, and Turner (1991) describe strategic reading as "a prime characteristic of expert readers because it is woven into the fabric of children's cognitive development and is necessary for success in school" (p. 609). They further describe these strategies in clusters.

- *Before reading:* previewing the text, making predictions
- *During reading:* identifying main ideas, making inferences, text inspection (looking forward and back in the text)
- *After reading:* summarizing, reflecting

If these are strategies, then what are skills? How are skills and strategies different? For years, educators have debated the difference between strategies and skills. During the 1980s and 1990s, skills got a bad reputation. Some equated skills with worksheets and isolated practice. Skills were equated with drill and kill, where as strategies were considered more long term and applied to continous text. As a result, some educators urged teachers to teach for strategies, as opposed to skills. Others worried that strategy instruction alone would not lead to skillful, engaged reading. The problem is that there was no consistent definition for skills and strategies. Thankfully, in an effort to clarify terms, Afflerbach, Pearson, and Paris (2008) have recently addressed this topic, and we have adopted their definitions. A strategy is a technique or process *consciously* employed by the reader to understand a text. Strategies change as the student reads different texts or for different purposes. Examples of strategic reading include "generating questions" or "making connections." Strategies are proven techniques used by readers to attain a reading goal, such as understanding the meaning of the text. Think of strategies as tools that a reader deliberately chooses to make meaning.

Afflerbach et al. (2008) note the two times when a strategy focus is especially useful. First, when students are apprenticing, or initially learning, then a strategy approach is useful. Of course, this requires explaining, modeling, and providing opportunities for practice with feedback. When Jessica was first learning from informational texts and we explained note taking to her, this strategy proved helpful. When Andrew was first learning to decode words, providing him with strategies such as sound–symbol correlation was critical.

Second, Afflerbach et al. (2008) note that strategies are also useful when readers encounter difficult texts. Recently, Nancy needed to learn more about Thomas Jefferson's legacy for a class she was teaching. She stumbled across a wonderful book about Jefferson's two families, one with his wife Martha that is common knowledge and well represented in the history books. The second family, much less commonly known, comes from Sally Hemings, an enslaved woman who had seven children with Jefferson after the death of Martha. Nancy could read all of the words in *Jefferson's Children: The Story of One American Family* (Lanier & Feldman, 2000), but she resorted to specific strategies to keep the information straight in her mind. She created a concept map, took notes, and made a timeline. There were simply too many facts, details, dates, and faces for her to remember them all. She consciously selected strategies (tools) to assist her in organizing the information.

Source: From *Jefferson's Children: The Story of One American Family* by Shannon Lanier and Jane Feldman, copyright © 2000 by Shannon Lanier and Jane Feldman. Used by permission of Random House Children's Books, a division of Random House, Inc.

In contrast, skills are *automatic* procedures that are product oriented, are habitual for competent readers, and are often tested on state assessments. Skills evolve from strategies that are practiced and refined over time, until they reach the point at which they become part of the flow of reading. It's a bit like learning a complicated dance. A novice dancer learns the steps through modeling and guided instruction by an expert. Through practice and multiple opportunities to experiment, the dancer is transformed. He is no longer simply executing a sequence of steps in the proper order. He moves from good to great because the steps are smooth and the artistry of the individual is allowed to emerge. A similar process occurs with readers who are taught strategies (the short-term direct instruction) with an eye toward consolidating these skills (the long-term purpose). This definition of reading skills may be different from the way it is used in some contexts.

A way to discern the difference between strategy and skills is to think of skills as "an acquired ability to perform well" (Harris & Hodges, 1995, p. 235), whereas a strategy is "a systematic plan, consciously adapted and monitored, to improve one's learning" (p. 244). A good reader knows how to consciously activate strategies to understand what is being read; a great reader has converted these strategies into a skillful execution and calls upon strategies when the reading becomes more difficult.

Building Great Readers Through Habits

We teach students strategies so that they can deliberately activate plans to solve problems they might encounter when reading a text. But our goal doesn't stop at the successful execution of a strategy. Just as a novice driver needs to be taught how to steer into a skid on an icy highway, readers need plans for getting through the tricky spots. A *great* reader has assimilated these strategies so that they become second nature. Just as a great driver can react correctly to the sudden skid, a great reader can negotiate the turns a text may take with a level of fluency and skill not seen in the novice. Habits are a routine, a way of life, not just something that is done to fulfill an assignment, or because now we're in English class, or because there's a summer reading list of 25 books.

Consider your own reading habits. Our guess is that you are able to become engrossed in a book without intentionally planning for strategies to support your comprehension. If the going gets tough, you consciously fall back on some strategies that have proven useful, such as tracking back to the place where you lost meaning. Yes, our students need to have a bag full of strategies that they can use when they encounter difficult texts. But most of the time, they should be skilled readers who automatically use what they know at the time they need it. Figure 1.1 provides a description of the differences between skills and strategies.

FIGURE 1.1 Comparing Skills and Strategies

Strategy	Skills
A conscious plan under the control of the reader.	An automatic procedure that readers use unconsciously.
Requires thought about which plan to use and when to use them.	Do not require thought, interpretation, or choice.
Are process-oriented, cognitive procedures the reader uses, generally unobservable in nature.	Are observable behaviors, found on taxonomies, skills tests, or answers to questions.
Instruction focuses on the reasoning process readers use as they interact with text.	Instruction focuses on repeated use until it becomes habitual.

Great Readers Display Habits

How is it that we get to the level of a great reader? That's the million-dollar question. We already touched on one point, gaining more precision in our teaching. In addition, our work with students suggests that we should focus on the habits that great readers use. Of course, these habits are comprised of a number of strategies, values, and beliefs. It's the goal that is different. We don't want to focus our students on strategies alone, but rather we want to focus on their enduring understanding. Based on our experiences, which include years of teaching, several research studies, graduate degrees, and reading hundreds of books and articles, we have identified seven habits that we have found useful in creating readers who are enthusiastic, engaged, and confident. These seven habits will each be considered in turn in this book.

- Great Readers See Themselves as Readers
- Great Readers Make Sense of Text
- Great Readers Use What They Know
- Great Readers Understand How Stories Work
- Great Readers Read to Learn
- Great Readers Monitor and Organize What They Read
- Great Readers Are Critical

We chose to focus on habits because Johnston (2004) cautioned us about telling students "this is what a good reader does," referring to specific strategies for specific chunks of texts, knowing that students might interpret this to mean that they are bad if they don't engage in that specific behavior for that specific piece of text. That's not to say that we don't help students understand what great readers do. Habits allow us to engage in inquiry with students—"Is this habit helpful?"—rather than tell them what they should do and when.

Importantly, these habits can't be simply taught in a few weeks. They require years of practice and attention to develop. As teachers, we must nourish these habits so they grow. Ideally, every year, starting in kindergarten, we need to model and teach our students these habits. As you'll see in the pages that follow, focusing attention on these habits results in students who read better and who read more—our criteria for success. In the pages that follow, you'll meet students we've had the pleasure to teach. You'll see how the relentless focus on habits results in motivated and independent readers who also perform well on assessment measures.

Professional Development

1. Dedicate a grade-level or faculty meeting to explore the question, "What characterizes a great reader?" Ask everyone to bring some artifacts or assessments of a student who they've identified as a great reader. This information could be a running record, journal entry, retelling, etc. In cross-grade-level groups, analyze the materials. Have each group create a definition of a great reader. See if the whole school can agree on a definition.
2. Ask teachers from different generations to share best practice reading instruction they learned when they were in education

school. Compare and contrast these different approaches to reading.

3. Ask each grade level to identify their benchmark expectations, skills, and strategies for a proficient reader. Display these expectations in a grade-level, developmental sequence. Are the expectations consistent across grades?

References

Afflerbach, P., Pearson, P. D., & Paris, S. (2008). Clarifying differences between reading skills and reading strategies. *The Reading Teacher. 61*, 364–373.

Collins, J. (2001). *Good to great: Why some companies make the leap . . . and others don't.* New York: HarperCollins.

Fullan, M., Hill, P., & Crévola, C. (2006). *Breakthrough.* Thousand Oaks, CA: Corwin.

Harvey, S., & Goudvis, A. (2007). *Strategies that work: Teaching comprehension to enhance understanding* (2nd ed.). York, ME: Stenhouse.

Harris, T. L., & Hodges, R. E. (1995). *The literacy dictionary: The vocabulary of reading and writing.* Newark, DE: International Reading Association.

Johnson, J. C. (2005). What makes a "good" reader? Asking students to define "good" readers. *The Reading Teacher, 58*, 766–773.

Johnston, P. H. (2004). *Choice words: How our language affects children's learning.* York, ME: Stenhouse.

Keene, E. O., & Zimmerman, S. (1997). *Mosaic of thought: Teaching comprehension in a reader's workshop.* Portsmouth, NH: Heinemann.

Lanier, S., & Feldman, J. (2000). *Jefferson's children: The story of one American family.* New York: Random House.

Myers, M. (1996). *Changing our minds: Negotiating English and literacy.* Urbana, IL: National Council of Teachers of English.

National Institute of Child Health and Human Development. (2000a). *Report of the National Reading Panel. Teaching children to read: An evidence-based assessment of the scientific research literature on reading and its implications for reading instruction* (NIH Publication No. 00-4769). Washington, DC: U.S. Government Printing Office.

National Institute of Child Health and Human Development. (2000b). *Report of the National Reading Panel. Teaching children to read: An evidence-based assessment of the scientific research literature on reading and its implications for reading instruction: Reports of the subgroups: Comprehension* (NIH Publication No. 00-4754). Washington, DC: U.S. Government Printing Office.

Paris, S. G., Wasik, B. A., & Turner, J. C. (1991). The development of strategic readers. In R. Barr, M. L. Kamil, P. Mosenthal, & P. D. Pearson (Eds.), *Handbook of reading research* (Vol. II, pp. 609–640). Mahwah, NJ: Lawrence A. Erlbaum.

Pinnell, G. S. (no date). *Matching books to readers.* Retrieved April 24, 2007, from teacher.scholastic.com/products/readingcounts/pdfs/matching_books.pdf

Pressley, M. (2000). What should comprehension instruction be the instruction of? In M. L. Kamil, P. B. Mosenthal, P. D. Pearson, & R. Barr (Eds.), *Handbook of reading research.* (Vol. 3, pp. 545–562). Mahwah, NJ: Erlbaum.

Texas Education Agency. (2002). *Comprehension instruction.* Austin, TX: Author.

CHAPTER 2

Great Readers See Themselves as Readers

Do you remember your first experiences with having books of your own? We do. Nancy remembers rushing home from first grade with her *Dick and Jane* reader clutched in her hand. Sister Dominic had told her that she could take it home only after she was able to read it independently. When that day came, it was momentous. Nancy still remembers reading to her parents about Puff the cat sitting on top of the television. Granted permission to transport that book from school to home encouraged Nancy to see herself as a reader.

Doug's story was different. A precocious reader, Doug was reading before he entered school. He remembers his mother giving him a new book, *The Cat in the Hat* (Seuss, 1967). As he read the words to his mother while she fixed dinner, she suddenly stopped what she was doing. She walked behind Doug to look at the words on the page. Grinning, he looked up and said, "Betcha didn't know I could do that!" Doug noticed that he could tackle a new book without an adult. That newfound independence let him see himself as a reader.

Many readers have a story to tell about an early experience with a favorite book, proudly carrying that book around the house, and on car trips, like a prized "security blanket." That moment can feel like a thunderbolt in the life of a child, one that builds his self-concept as an independent and competent person. Every child needs those moments, the sooner the better. Our classrooms are built on helping our students see themselves as readers from the very beginning. Here, we are not equating "seeing yourself as a reader" with "being able to read." Throughout the grades, our first job each school year is to build the habit of seeing oneself as a reader. This designation isn't based on a report card grade, or the color of the dot on the spine of the book, and definitely not about being in the top-level reading group. It's about internalizing a belief that you have been welcomed into the most inclusive club in the world—the world of fellow readers.

Think of the sense of community you feel in the company of readers. We quiet our voices when we enter a library, aware of the hushed atmosphere that shelters us from the cacophony outside. We step gingerly around other citizen-readers as we make our way to our favorite section of the neighborhood bookstore. Little conversation is needed—we signal to one another with small smiles and a shift of our eyes as we reach for that new book with the intriguing cover. A glance up on a subway train reveals another traveler reading the magazine we're holding, and a look of recognition passes between them. "Ahh," we think, "he's reading the same words I am." That sense of fellowship among readers transcends gender, age, and interest. This is the fellowship, the atmosphere, the community, we need to create in our classrooms.

We enter a bookstore or a library because we want to read. No one's forcing us to be there; it's not a homework assignment. We are motivated to read. There has been quite a bit of research on the importance of motivation in reading. John Guthrie and Allan Wigfield (2000) describe children whose "devotion to reading spans across time, transfers to a variety of genres, and culminates in valued leaning outcomes" (p. 403). The beginning of the school year is the perfect time to start building a motivation to read. Motivation isn't a strategy, it's a habit, and like other habits it needs to be cultivated. We know those motivated readers when we see them. There's a book squirreled away in the backpack, one that we didn't assign. There's the transported look on the face of a child who may be physically in room 408, but is living at that

John Graham

moment inside the rabbit warren of the Cottontail family. There's the boy with skateboarding magazines spread across the school library table, devouring every article that mentions Tony Hawk. There's the student reading webpage after webpage to find out about a favorite pop star. Clearly, these students see themselves as readers. But what of those who don't exhibit that "devotion to reading"? Could it be that they feel left out of the fellowship, marginalized to the outer edges of the reading community? How do we let them know the door is open for them to enter?

We trust them. We trust them to handle books, even when the fingers might be sticky. We trust them to talk about books, even when the conversation seems to always get back to Captain Underpants. We trust them to choose books, even when we secretly worry that one of their choices might be too hard for them right now. And we trust them to read genres that might not appear in the state standards. All of these actions build habituation—growing accustomed to the notion that they are readers, and that their reading is valued, because *they* are valued.

HELPING STUDENTS SEE THEMSELVES AS READERS

In the sections that follow, we'll focus on four areas that ensure students develop this habit.

1. Taking Care of Books
2. Choosing Books
3. Knowing Yourself as a Reader
4. Building Reading Stamina

Over time, and with feedback and support from a caring teacher, our students will see themselves as readers.

Taking Care of Books

The beginning of the year is the time to teach procedures and rituals that build our classroom community. Consistent with this priority, we introduce the habit of seeing oneself as a reader with instruction on taking care of books. These lessons on book handling provide us with the opportunity to teach classroom procedures while also introducing literacy content. This ensures that from the start of the year, our students are learning about the value of books, as well as their competence in handling them. Students who perceive themselves as being competent at tasks are more likely to be successful academically (Bandura, 1989).

We find that teaching about the value of books is something that comes as naturally as breathing, and we suspect that other teachers feel this way, too. Each day at the beginning of the school year we bring in our own favorite books from childhood and talk for a few minutes about why they are meaningful to us. Nancy shares her *Madeline* books by Ludwig Bemelmans (1998) and tells her young students about why the girl who wasn't afraid of anything made her feel a little less afraid. Adam reads aloud *The Teacher from the Black Lagoon* (Thaler, 1989) and reassures his students that he's not a monster. Doug brings in his dog-eared copy of *Hatchet* by Gary Paulsen (1999) and tells his older students about reading the book for the first time as an adult when he was on a plane headed for Alaska (a bit unsettling for him!). Students are encouraged to bring in favorites of their own and of their family members. One of our first homework assignments is to interview your family members about their treasured books. Eight-year-old Regina told us one day, in wide-eyed amazement, about the ancient family Bible her great-grandmother hauled out from the top shelf of the bedroom closet. Eleven-year-old Arturo proudly shared his collection of *lucha libre* wrestling magazines, and his favorite *luchador*, Juventud. (Arturo has taught us quite a bit about Mexican wrestling.) These "treasured book" talks occur several times each week throughout the year and can be done at any time by either the teacher or a student. We want our students to see books as treasures and see favorite authors as friends.

When students see books as "treasures," they are motivated to take care of them. One of our favorite ways to introduce taking care of books is to look at the ways books are constructed. Our older students learn about ancient bookbinding methods such as scrolls and Coptic bindings, as well as modern techniques using glue or thread. Used bookstores are a treasure trove for acquiring inexpensive examples of leather-bound, hand-tooled, pressboard, and fabric-covered books. We fill a table with dozens of old books and allow our students to thumb through them.

One of our early journal entries invites students to choose a book and live with it for a few days, then write an imagined life. Who owned it? How did they acquire it? Why was it important to this person? We've been amazed by the detective work some of our students have engaged in. Marco, a fourth-grade student, noticed the bookplate on the inside cover and wrote a tale of a grandfather who gave the book to his youngest grandchild on the eve of her first day of school. He explained that the margin notes in different handwritings were the product of two generations of readers. We have found that when students are asked to immerse themselves in the tactile sensations of a book, they get a glimpse of the history it carries forward from reader to reader.

Our youngest readers make very simple books for themselves, and we give them a tour of the variety of books available to them. In addition, we develop a set of rules for book treatment. The rules are pretty consistent from year to year, and usually follow these themes.

- Make sure your hands are clean.
- Don't put the book down on anything that's wet or messy.
- Keep the book flat, and don't bend it backward.
- Turn the pages carefully.
- No writing in the book!

Of course, little hands take their toll on best-loved books, and accidents do happen. Our students usually feel terrible when a book is damaged, and we don't want to make them feel any worse. We keep a jar labeled "Random Acts of Book Kindnesses" in the classroom with three-by-five-inch cards filled with suggestions, such as *Look for stray books that need to be put away* and *Make a new cover for one that is getting tattered.* We keep lots of brown paper shopping bags on hand so that our students can make a simple protective cover anytime they need one. We also cut old manila folders into three-by-eight-inch strips for bookmarks. Readers decorate their bookmarks and we reinforce the use of them to protect the binding and make it easier to resume reading.

Choosing Books

Think about the ways that you go about choosing books to read. Getting recommendations from friends, reading reviews, and browsing in bookstores and libraries. These are the same strategies we model and teach our students. Young readers need to develop a sense of self as readers so they can choose books that meet their purposes. The ability to choose books for one's self is critical because it engages students in the world of reading (Fresch, 1995). Choice is an assertion of independence, essential for students as they take charge of their own reading. Closely related to the concept of choice is an understanding of oneself as a reader. Knowledge of one's preferences for topics, settings, and authors is essential in building lifelong readers (Baker, Dreher, & Guthrie, 2000). We see teaching students to choose books as a way to build their independence. Remember Doug's realization that he didn't need an adult around in order to read? What a powerful insight. We want our students to know, right from Day 1, that they don't need someone else to mediate their reading. In our classrooms, choosing books is more than selecting the "just right book" (though that's important, too). Choosing one's own book is an empowering act, one made by learners confident in their ability to know themselves as readers.

Learning how to choose books for oneself is not as simple as teaching students a few lessons on the five-finger method and then turning them loose in the stacks. Great readers know that they are constantly evolving as readers, and that their ability, tastes, and interests change. Doug and Nancy didn't know a single thing about graphic novels (books that look like comic books, but aren't) until Emilio introduced them to us. He told us they were different from comic books because the story is self-contained, not serialized like comic books. Nancy had only read *Archie* and a few others during a short-lived phase in fourth grade, while Doug spent more quality time with *Richie Rich* and *Spiderman*. Emilio taught us about *Bone* (Smith, 2004), a 1,300-page (yes, you read that correctly) single story following the adventures of the Bone cousins, Fone Bone, Smiley Bone, and Phoney Bone, who have been run out of Boneville. This is *The Odyssey* for the grade school set, and we would never have guessed that Emilio had the stamina for it. We immediately got ourselves copies (heavy lifting) and Nancy discovered that her capacity for corny jokes had not diminished, while Doug learned that there might be something to this genre. Fast-forward a few years, and you'll find us to be prodigious consumers of graphic novels. We get the occasional odd look from a sullen teenager when they see us searching in the Graphic Novels section of our local bookstore, but we're there because a 10-year-old boy taught us something we didn't know about ourselves.

So how do you get your students to choose books for themselves? First, of course, is the book flood. There needs to be so many different kinds of books in your classroom that no one could ever get away with the excuse that "there's nothing to read." Beyond that, you need to talk about books, as well as why you chose a book for yourself. Did a friend recommend it? Maybe you saw a great book review and thought, "Hmm, that reminds me of another book I liked. Maybe I'll pick that one up." Because great readers understand themselves, they also know that not every book is a good fit for every reader. Our students do book talks every week in the Literacy Lounge (really, it's just that the lights are turned down in the classroom and we throw tablecloths over the tables). They meet with two or three other readers and describe the book, why

Source: Out From Boneville © 1991, 1992, 2005 Jeff Smith. Bone® is a registered trademark of Jeff Smith. Used by permission of Cartoon Books, Inc.

they chose it, and a recommendation. Here's the important part—they also need to state who *wouldn't* like this book. We hear students say things like, "This isn't a good book for people who don't like stories about robots" or "Don't pick this book if you like a fast start to a book." Perhaps our favorite comment came from kindergartner Rachelle, a girl with pigtails and missing teeth, who leaned across the table to her partners and whispered, "Don't read this if you don't like a perfect book!" We'll keep working with Rachelle, but the point is that reading is a community act. Even when we are lost in a story, there's still a part of our brain that knows others have read this, and that others will read this, and will get lost in it just as we have, or who will put it down 25 pages in and never pick it up again. Reading may be a solitary act, but it is one that is performed daily in communion with others.

Choosing books also means having a few tools to make choices rapidly. That means that the young ones can figure out if a book is too hard by using the "five-finger rule." Show your students how to read a page and keep track of the number of unfamiliar words. If you use all five fingers before you get to the bottom of the page, it might be too hard. We also model previewing strategies quite a bit. We look at titles together, as well as illustrations and other eye-catching features. We also show them how to read the inside flap of the cover, or scan the back of the book for an engaging summary. Even though these tools alone can't guarantee a good fit, they work well when combined with lots of opportunities to choose books.

Knowing Yourself as a Reader

This is really an extension of choosing books, because a reader's ability to choose successfully is predicated on understanding one's preferences and intentions. This means noticing the things that capture your interest, pique your curiosity, and cause you to question. It also means drawing upon past reading experiences in order to inform future aims. Student interest in elementary school is a tricky business because it shifts like quicksilver. We've found that it isn't helpful to survey them once at the beginning of the year because the shelf life is so short. Nancy recalls an event early in her teaching career when she was teaching second grade. Michael had expressed tremendous (one might say obsessive) interest in fire trucks. She set about finding everything she could on fire trucks, and even called the local fire station to request pamphlets and any other ephemera they had on hand. This took weeks, but at her next reading conference with Michael she proudly shared the fruit of her efforts. He leafed through them unenthusiastically, then said, "Don't you have anything on Nile monitor lizards?"

A good rule of thumb is that the younger the reader, the more often we need to check in with their interests. A number of good interest surveys are available to teachers, and we have a few favorites. For older readers, we like the one produced by the American Library Association, and first developed by Denice Hildebrandt (2001). It is available online at http://www.ala.org/ala/yalsa/teenreading/tipsenc/reading_interest_survey.pdf. We don't ask them to fill it out over and over; we keep it with our reading conference materials and revisit it with them from time to time to see how their interests are changing. Importantly, we want them to notice how their tastes are changing, and why. Younger students need something a bit simpler, so we adapted the work of Donna Skolnick (2000) for our own purposes. It has some items about their reading habits and attitudes, and we find this is more useful to conduct face-to-face so we can get a bit more conversation going. We have included our reading interest survey in Figure 2.1.

FIGURE 2.1 Reading Interest Survey

Name: ______________________ Date: _______________

Please circle the answer that is best for you.

Reading Survey Questions

1. I like to choose my own books to read.

   Always *Sometimes* *Never*

2. I can usually find a good book to read.

   Yes *No*

3. I like to read chapter books.

   Yes *Not yet*

4. I read at home

   Every day *Every few days* *Not if I can help it*

5. At home I like to read

   In bed *On the floor* *In a comfortable chair*

6. The kinds of books I like to read include:

   _________ Chapter books _________ Nonfiction
   _________ Books with pictures _________ Animal stories
   _________ Jokes and riddle books _________ Mysteries
   _________ Sports books _________ Funny stories

   Other____

7. Books and authors I have read:

   ____

Source: Adaptation printed by permission from *More than meets the eye: How relationships enhance literacy learning* by Donna Skolnick. Copyright © 2000 by Donna Skolnick. Published by Heinemann, a division of Reed Elsevier, Inc., Portsmouth, NH. All rights reserved.

The issue of conferring is an important one. Without regular contact with our students in face-to-face interactions, we find that we quickly lose touch with them. Trying to keep up with their rapid developmental and cognitive growth is daunting. Lucy Calkins (2005) has taught us quite a bit about the need to stay in constant communication with them individually, even if it is just for a few minutes at a time. Regularly scheduled reading conferences are a part of that formula, but we have found that much can be gained from planning spontaneous interactions. This sounds like an oxymoron, this planned spontaneity, but we are referring to constructing good questions in advance so that when the opportunities occur, you're prepared. Nancie Atwell (2007) has done a wonderful job of cataloging questions she asks as she "roams among readers" and we now keep these on a clipboard to remind us of deep questions we can ask our students to help them understand who they are as readers. Some are procedural, such as asking about where they are in the book, but many others cause students to notice things about themselves, such as inviting them to compare the current reading to other books they have read by the same author, or why they chose to reread a book. These questions are listed in Figure 2.2.

Knowing yourself as a reader is more than just knowing what you like, it's also knowing what you don't like, and why it's not a good match for you. Insight into what doesn't work is a powerful example of metacognitive awareness, that knowledge of how and when you learn. When Angelina can tell Doug that she "doesn't want to read anymore books where the dog dies at the end," she is signaling to herself and to him that those heartbreaking endings are too emotionally difficult right now. When Michael went on to explain to Nancy that "fire trucks are for little kids," she noticed that his shifting tastes paralleled his developmental growth. We're not opposed to students abandoning books, because every book isn't a home run for every reader. However, we want to know why they abandoned it, because it provides both of us—teacher and reader—with insight into interests and preferences.

Building Reading Stamina

Of course, choice and preference are of little consequence if a reader lacks the persistence to finish a book. We want our students to be constantly evolving as readers. We want our youngest readers to move from picture books to transitional chapter books, to longer chapter books. During this unit, we have conversations about rereading favorite books, reading every day, and looking forward to the next book to be read (Calkins, 2001).

Each student in our classes sets goals for daily reading. By fourth grade, we want them to be reading at least 25 chapter books a year; for younger students who are reading short picture books, we aim for 100 annually. Reading volume plays an important role in acquiring literacy, as shown through studies by Keith Stanovich, Anne Cunningham, and other researchers. A simple reading log is sufficient, because we don't want to turn this into a laborious effort that turns them off to the act of reading. All we ask for is the

FIGURE 2.2 Questions to Ask as You Roam Among Readers

Always:
What page are you on?
Mostly:
What do you think so far?
How is it?
What's happening now?
And also:
Any surprises so far?
How did you feel when you got to the part about ____________ ?
Main character queries:
Who's the main character in this one?
What's the main character like?
What's his problem, or hers?
How's the character development in general? Are you convinced?
Author queries:
Who wrote this one?
What do you think of the writing so far?
Do you know anything special about the author?
Any theories about why he or she might have written this?
How is it so far, compared to his or her other books?
Critical queries:
What genre is this one?
How is it so far, compared with other books about ____________ ?
Is it plausible?
How's the pace?
What's the narrative voice? How's that working for you?
What do you think of the dialogue/format/length of chapters/flashbacks/inclusion of poems/diction choices/author's experiments with ____________, and so on (depending on the book)?
When it's a page-turner:
What's making this a page-turner for you? What are you noticing? For example, is it formulaic—easy for you to predict?
Process inquiries:
Why did you decide to read this one?
I can't believe how much you read last night. Tell me about that.
Why did you decide to reread this one?
Where did you find this book?
When there's no zone:
Is this book taking you into the reading zone?
Why do you think it's taking you so long to read this?
Can you skim the parts that drag—the descriptions, for example?
Are you confused because it's hard to understand the language, or because you can't tell what's going on?
Are you considering abandoning this book? Because if you're not hooked by now, that's more than okay. You can always come back to it someday.
Do you want to skim to find out what happens, or even read the ending, then move on to a better book?
What's on your someday list?
Do you know what other book I think you might like?
Finis:
Now that you've finished it, what would you rate this one?
Is this one worthy of a booktalk? Do you want to schedule a talk for tomorrow?
What are you planning on reading next?

Source: Atwell, N. (2007). *The reading zone: How to help students become skilled, passionate, habitual, critical readers.* New York: Scholastic.

Patrick White/Merrill

title, author, and a short evaluation. We have smiley faces on the kindergarten reading logs, and the older students rate it on a scale of 1 to 5.

1 I didn't like it and wouldn't recommend it to anyone else.

2 I didn't like it, but someone else might.

3 It was OK, but I can't get excited.

4 I liked it and would recommend it to others.

5 This could be one of my favorites this year.

This quantitative data is coupled with a single word: *Because*. . . One of our colleagues from Michigan, Theresa Czarnopys, walks around her classroom with a sign that reads *Because*. . . to remind her students that an answer isn't complete without a rationale. We ask them to write a few sentences about their reasoning. This becomes a topic for future conferring as we meet with them individually to discuss their reading habits. There's no book report, mostly because we don't like to do them either, but also because they interfere with real reading. We treasure our time spent with our friends in our Tuesday night book club, and we're very thankful that we don't have to prepare a book report in advance. Doug might have quit if he had to write a book report on *Blindness* by Jose Saramago (1998), and that was one of his favorite book club choices ever.

In addition to volume, building stamina means expanding the range of genres one reads. We talk about our "reading diets" and draw analogies to the food pyramid. Just as physical health is enhanced by daily consumption of fruits, vegetables,

Source: From *Love That Dog*, by Sharon Creech. Copyright © 2001 by Sharon Creech. Used by permission of HarperCollins.

grains, dairy, and meat, so is the reading health of a great reader. Primary students learn about basic genres such as informational, poetry, biography, folktales, animal stories, and realistic fiction. This is further expanded each year as we look closely at science fiction, fantasy, how-to manuals, graphic novels, historical fiction, and so on. Students note in their reading log the genre they would assign this book, which is a trickier proposition than one would think. What genre is *Dan the Flying Man* (Cowley, 2001) anyway?

Some of our colleagues ask students to graph their reading diet monthly so that they can create a visual representation of the types of books they're reading (and not reading). We think this is a great idea. We don't have a prescribed formula for genres—no "Noah's Ark" proclamations about two of each, or whatever. Instead, we try to consider the reader as well as the genre in making recommendations. Marcello, a student of Doug's, suggested that everyone should have a "no-thank-you helping" of each genre, and the idea has stuck. Think of the countless nights you spent as a child at the dinner table while some well-meaning adult tried to cajole you into eating all your lima beans. No bribe, guilt, or threat existed that would ever make you like lima beans. A "no-thank-you helping" is a small serving, not too distasteful, that would have satisfied your mother or father and wouldn't have killed you. We occasionally ask our students for "no-thank-you" recommendations for others who view certain genres the same way we saw those lima beans. *Love That Dog* by Sharon Creech (2001), for example, has become a "no-thank-you helping" for reluctant poetry readers because it's short and is on a topic that is universally appealing. We've known quite a few readers who have changed their minds over time about genres, just like we have about lima beans.

It is important to acknowledge that reading stamina, like physical fitness, is built over time and requires a commitment of time. It isn't realistic to expect that students will meet their reading goals if time is set aside only once a week. Dick Allington 2006 reminds us that reclaiming time for reading means looking closely at the ways in which time is used and then being brave enough to restructure it. That means minimizing disruptions, carving out longer blocks of instruction, and reducing the kinds of episodic literacy that requires students to only read a few sentences before the activity changes. Allington calls this "reading interruptus" and notes that

> In the world outside of school people read at least whole chapters and whole articles in one sitting. They write complete letters to the editor, persuasive essays, shopping lists, and reports as a single episode, not as a series of five- to ten-minute activities; it takes time to read deeply and to write thoughtfully. (p. 54)

A final aspect of building reading stamina is having a plan for the *next* book. A hallmark of a great reader is that there's an endless supply of next books—a huge stack on the nightstand, a pile next to the coffee table in the family room. Doug has a sign over his office that reads, "So many books, so little time" and nothing could be truer about a person who seems himself as a reader. Our kindergarten students have a book basket on their tables for the "next book." They are reminded to replenish it as they work their way through the books they're reading. Older students keep a book plan with a list of titles they have either seen or heard someone else talk about. April, a fifth-grade student, told us that she thinks of her book plan as being "like NetFlix [the video rental service]. You have to keep a list of movies in the queue so they know what to send you next." We love that she knows the word *queue* and that she made this connection to other aspects of her life. Maybe we'll start calling them BookFlix.

MOVING FROM GOOD TO GREAT

We chose to talk about this habit first because it is the catalyst for all the others that follow. It's difficult to get children to use what they know, or read critically, if they doubt their own worthiness. We can think of few things that can more negatively impact motivation than a secret belief that one is a pretender to the act of reading. Struggling readers are at great risk of this. They furtively glance around at their classmates and wonder, "What do they know that I don't?"

But we also worry about the students who can read, but choose not to. They also have an insistent voice inside their head saying, "What does everyone else see in this that I don't?" These inner voices work on a child's sense of self-efficacy and undermine what we're trying to do—create lifelong readers. Childhood is about becoming increasingly independent in all aspects of life. The exhilaration of riding a bike for the first time without training wheels, or being allowed to cross the street alone, or staying in the house without a babysitter are milestones in the lives of children. How do we create these exhilarating moments in our classroom? By welcoming them into the reading club, and letting them see that their ideas matter. After all, if they can see themselves as readers, what else might they recognize in themselves? Notice and encourage the following behaviors.

Does the student:

Take Care of Books

- Show care when picking up and opening a book?
- Put a book away in the correct place?

Choose Books

- Identify favorite books and authors?
- Preview a book by examining the title, cover, and content?
- Name several sources of information for finding books?

- Seek out reading material that is different from what he or she usually chooses?
- Have a purpose for reading and use that purpose to make an appropriate choice?
- Have a balanced reading diet from a variety of genres?

Know Self as a Reader

- Recognize a book that is too easy or too hard?
- Use the five-finger rule to determine if a book is "just right"?
- Select a new book based on personal preferences?

Build Reading Stamina

- Identify goals for becoming a better reader and "I can. . ." ways of achieving those goals?
- Practice reading in order to build up reading stamina?
- Set goals for becoming a better reader?
- Make an effort to read independently?

Professional Development

1. Describe one of your earliest memories with a favorite book. What made the experience so special?
2. Devote a faculty meeting to looking at reading logs. Ask each teacher to bring a reading log assigned at his or her grade level. Post the reading logs on a wall, in grade-level sequence. What do you notice? Do the expectation from grade to grade make sense?
3. Invite older students to visit your classroom and talk about their reading diet.
4. Work with your librarian to create a "No Thank You" display in your school library. Rotate the responsibility for display each month, assigning a different class or a different grade.
5. Bring completed reading surveys to a faculty meeting. Can you identify any developmental patterns in reading interests?
6. Invite a local used-book seller to a "back-to-school night." Create a culture in your school and parent community that values old books. Hold the book version of the "The Antique Road School." Ask families to bring and display their oldest book.

References

Allington, R. A. (2006). *What really matters for struggling readers: Designing research-based programs* (2nd ed.). Boston: Pearson Allyn & Bacon.

Atwell, N. (2007). *The reading zone: How to help students become skilled, passionate, habitual, critical readers.* New York: Scholastic.

Baker, L., Dreher, M. J., & Guthrie, J. T. (2000). Why teachers should promote reading engagement. In L. Baker, M. J. Dreher, & J. T. Guthrie (Eds.), *Engaging young readers* (pp. 1–16). New York: Guilford.

Bandura, A. (1989). Human agency in social cognitive theory. *American Psychologist, 44*, 1175–1184.

Bemelmans, L. (1998). *Madeline.* New York: Puffin.

Calkins, L. M. (2001). *The art of teaching reading.* New York: Longman.

Calkins, L. M. (2005). *One to one: The art of conferring with young writers.* Portsmouth, NH: Heinemann.

Cowley, J. (2001). *Dan, the flying man.* Auckland, NZ: McGraw-Hill Shortland Publications.

Creech, S. (2001). *Love that dog.* New York: HarperCollins.

Fresch, M. (1995). Self-selection of early literacy learners. *The Reading Teacher, 49*(3), 220–227.

Guthrie, J. T., & Wigfield, A. (2000). Engagement and motivation in reading. In M. L. Kamil, P. B. Mosenthal, P. D. Pearson, & R. Barr (Eds.), *Handbook of reading research* (Vol. III, pp. 403–424). Mahwah, NJ: Lawrence Erlbaum.

Hildebrandt, D. (2001, Fall). But there's nothing good to read. *Media Spectrum: The Journal for Library Media Specialists in Michigan,* 34–37.

Paulsen, G. (1999). *Hatchet.* New York: Aladdin.

Saramago, J. (1998). *Blindness.* New York: Harcourt Brace.

Seuss, D. (1967). *The cat in the hat.* New York: Random House.

Skolnick, D. (2000). *More than meets the eye: How relationships enhance literacy learning.* Portsmouth, NH: Heinemann.

Smith, J. (2004). *Bone.* Columbus, OH: Cartoon Books.

Thaler, M. (1989). *The teacher from the black lagoon.* New York: Scholastic.

CHAPTER 3

Great Readers Make Sense of Text

Great readers make sense of text. Their goal is not simply to say the words or to decode the print. Of course, being able to decode the symbols on the page is a critical part of making sense of the text; it's just not enough. In other words, phonics is necessary but not sufficient. Similarly, fluency, reading fast enough, recognizing the words, and keeping information in your mind is also important, but not sufficient. Readers need to make sense of what they read and they do so by mobilizing literacy processes simultaneously.

Unfortunately, we know a number of students who are word callers (or "phonicators," as some say). They can slowly decode the majority of words on a page, but have no idea what they've just read. They have not developed automaticity—they are so focused on pedaling the bike, they can't enjoy the scenery. They also cannot intentionally call upon plans for enhancing their understanding. In short, they are not good readers, much less great readers.

Third-grader Anthony was a student who believed the goal of reading was to correctly name each of the words. He struggled daily to sound out words, without monitoring what he was reading. When we first met Anthony, reading a paragraph and then retelling it was very difficult. For example, after struggling to read, "Good friends come in all shapes and sizes," from *Owen & Mzee: The True Story of a Remarkable Friendship* (Hatkoff, Hatkoff, & Kahumbu, 2006), Anthony was unable to answer the question, "Who are the friends the author is talking about?" or "What do they mean by 'all shapes and sizes'?" Although the sentence seems very simple, and the wonderful photograph should have helped him comprehend, he was unable to do so. His cognitive energy was spent on decoding and he didn't have the reserves for comprehension. The text made little sense to him. Of course, we have all had experiences in which our reading energy was spent and we didn't understand the text. For example, Doug was asked to read a legal brief about grade-level retention and social promotion. Although interested and opinionated

Source: Cover photograph copyright © 2005 by Peter Greste from *Owen & Mzee: The True Story of a Remarkable Friendship* by Isabella Hatkoff et al., Scholastic Inc./Scholastic Press. Reprinted by permission.

about this particular topic, Doug spent a great deal of energy focused on the sentence structure and legal terminology used by the lawyer and thus had a hard time making sense of the brief. He sought guidance and support from a lawyer, someone who was much more experienced with this genre.

Anthony also needed help. Like Doug, he needed modeling and guidance. To move beyond the status of a word caller, Anthony needed experiences interacting with text at his reading level. He also needed to talk about texts with his peers.

MAKING SENSE OF TEXT

Most importantly, though, what Anthony needed to move forward in his reading was some understanding of meaning making. He needed to become a good reader who used a number of strategies intentionally, before he could become a great reader with skills and automaticity. Anthony needed instruction in the following four elements great readers use to gain meaning from text.

1. Summarizing and Synthesizing
2. Asking Questions
3. Clarifying
4. Making Predictions

It is no coincidence that these four habits are the same ones used in reciprocal teaching (Palincsar & Brown, 1984). We selected reciprocal teaching as the organizer for this habit because we have effectively used this robust instructional strategy to move students from strategy to habit. However, these great readers engage in these habits individually and in combination with one another, based upon cognitive demand of the text. Therefore, these habits, and this chapter, are not just about reciprocal teaching as an instructional approach. Rather, we have used the elements of reciprocal teaching to frame our discussion about four essential areas of reading comprehension. In this chapter, we will also discuss related comprehension strategies not directly associated with reciprocal teaching.

Reciprocal teaching is "an instructional procedure in which teachers and students take turns leading discussions about a shared text. The purpose of these discussions is to achieve joint understanding of the text through the flexible application of four comprehension strategies: prediction, clarification, summarization, and question generation" (Palincsar & Klenk, 1991, p. 116). Each of these specific strategies is complex and students need multiple opportunities to apply them and discuss their use. Annemarie Palincsar and Ann Brown, the original developers of the approach, estimated that students require approximately 20 days of practice in order to become proficient with the process (1984). We know we may sound like your piano teacher, but it's true: Practice is important. Attention to the initial learning phase of this process pays off later because it allows students to turn their attention to the ways in which they are making sense of the text, not just the mechanics of applying the strategy. Palincsar and Brown have been clear that the order in which readers engage in these comprehension strategies is less important than their increasing ability to be able to activate the *right* strategy for the time.

These four comprehension strategies have been artfully combined in reciprocal teaching (for implementation ideas see Oczkus, 2003). They can also be used individually to provide students with practice and application. We'll consider each of these in greater detail below.

Summarizing and Synthesizing

As readers, we regularly summarize as we read. We don't wait until the end of a particular piece of text to summarize; our brains do this as a way to store information. We can't remember every single detail from the text; instead, we search for lasting impressions or big ideas. Unfortunately, some struggling readers haven't been let in on this trick. They think that they are responsible for remembering everything that the author wrote. Doug remembers asking Tia, a fourth-grader, to summarize several pages from *Exploring the Titanic* (Ballard, 1988). She spewed forth a list of isolated facts about the number of passengers, the menu of the last meal, and so forth. While she demonstrated her ability to recall bits of information, Tia didn't understand the key ideas from the text. When asked for a single summary sentence, Tia responded, "But there is too much to say it in one sentence! I don't know what the author wants me to learn."

One of the ways that readers make sense of text is through summarizing. This can be a point of confusion for some students and teachers, who equate summarizing with providing a summary. Summarizing is an *ongoing* reading strategy—it's when you periodically pause as you are reading to restate what you just read. Usually, people don't verbalize these summaries aloud. A summary is a written or oral statement that describes the key points of a text. The ability to provide a summary is an outgrowth of summarizing. Notice how we highlighted the word *ongoing*. Poor readers don't summarize at all, good readers wait until the end of the reading to summarize, and great readers summarize throughout their reading (Paris, Wasik, & Turner, 1991). Anthony rarely, if ever, summarized. When we asked him to, he either gave us a blank stare or provided a few random facts. Teaching summarizing improves memory and recall of details, as well as main ideas discussed in the text (Armbruster, Anderson, & Ostertag, 1987).

There are a number of effective ways for helping students learn to summarize and synthesize information. We've used summary frames during the modeling phase of instruction, which typically include a series of questions that direct student attention to specific content (Marzano, Pickering, & Pollock, 2001). For example, following a number of examples through modeling, students were provided a summary frame for use with a primary source document. The frame

FIGURE 3.1 Summary Frame

_____________ is one of the characters in the story. _______ is ________________ and lives _______________
At the beginning of the story, _________________ is _________________, but ___________________ who
_______________________ _________________ _________________ faces a problem when __________
____.
____.
____
attempts to solve the problem by ____
but ____. Finally, ____________
is able to solve the problem by ____.
At the end of the story, ___________________________ has learned that ______________________________ if
____, then ____.

FIGURE 3.2 Student Writing Based on Writing Frame

Jeffrey is one of the Characters in the story. He is a boy and lives in Two Mills. At the beginning of the story, he is homeless, but Amanda who is his friend lets him live there. Jeffrey faces a problem when he runs away again and lives at the zoo. A man named Earl takes him home to live. Then Earl dies because he is old. Jeffrey attempts to solve the problem by running away again because he wants to die, but the McNabbs take him to their bad house. Finally, Jeffrey is able to solve the problem by helping them to be better people. At the end of the story, Jefrey has learned that friends care if you trust them, then they will take care of you.

directed them to identify key phrases from the text to include in their summary. Importantly, over time students internalize these writing frames and begin to use them on their own (Graff & Birkenstein, 2006), and such devices are not necessary, or even advisable, as readers become more comfortable with the strategy. A sample summary frame focusing on character analysis can be found in Figure 3.1. A sample student response, based on *Maniac Magee* (Spinelli, 1999), can be found in Figure 3.2. Figure 3.3 includes a sample summary frame for an informational text.

Summary frames are not the only way to help students develop this skill. Teaching students to take notes and to create visual representations of the text are also effective in helping students identify big ideas or key points. What these all

FIGURE 3.3 Compare/Contrast Informational Text Summary Frame

___________ and __________ are alike and are different in several ways. First, they are alike because ________ but they are different because ___________. Secondly, __________ is ____________ while ________ is _________. Finally, __________ and ____________ are alike because ______________. But, they are different because ______________.

have in common is that readers must pause periodically while reading to monitor and summarize. Great readers do this automatically.

Nancy keeps a visual diary of the things she reads, filling the pages with icons and sketches. Adam takes notes in a journal while he reads. Doug just writes in the book. Pick up any book in Doug's house and you'll find marginalia, notes to self in the back cover, and a number of underlined words and phrases. For example, Doug recently read *The Long Tail: Why the Future of Business Is Selling Less of More* (Anderson, 2006), a book about the impact that niche markets will experience as a result of the global economy, the Internet, and the increased access people have to information. As a nonbusiness person, Doug had difficulty summarizing and applying the information he was reading. However, he was interested in reading the book because Nicki asked him about the implications the long tail might have on students' future reading habits as it becomes easier for books in electronic form to be kept in database inventories. If you flipped through Doug's copy of the book, you'd find his attempts to summarize and synthesize written right inside the book. For example, on the pages where the author describes i-Tunes, Doug wrote, "Digital storage reduces shelf space requirements thus buyers can find more stuff to buy." Of course, the author didn't say this and it's a bit simplistic, but writing this short summary as he was reading helped Doug understand what he was reading, and later when he was skimming through the book, it helped him find the information and recall what he was thinking. We will explore more note-taking techniques in Chapter 7. Identify ways you, a proficient reader, summarize and synthesize, and share these examples with your students.

We're not suggesting that students write in their books, but that they benefit from being taught about summarizing and how this strategy helps them make sense of texts. When they summarize and synthesize information, students engage in a number of critical and creative thinking skills that help them learn, remember, and engage.

Asking Questions

We've come to understand that generating questions is much more important than simply answering questions from the teacher. Why? Because if you generate an authentic question, something you really want to know, you are motivated to search for the answer. And when you are searching, you are learning. The inquiry itself becomes the motivation. How many times have you had a question about something and then read to find out the answer? This is a major reason why Internet search engines are so popular—they help people find answers to their questions. Nancy was on a trip to Toronto, Canada. To pass the time on the plane, she started reading her guidebook to Toronto. She kept coming across the words *provinces* and *territories*. Nancy wondered about the difference between the two. She asked others traveling with her about this (we didn't know) and so she read more to find out. She e-mailed her answer to the people she asked to keep them informed: "Territories do not have inherent jurisdiction (provinces do). This would be equivalent to our system of state governments that have laws that differ from federal law. Territories only have federal law for governance." Stephanie Harvey aptly conveys our passion for questions when she notes, "Live the questions. Value the questions. They are the doors to understanding" (1998, p. 31). When our students are brimming with questions, they will read to find the answers. Share your questions and your search for the answers with your students—build the passion.

Readers benefit from learning how to generate their own questions about the text, both questions that help them monitor their understanding and that help them clarify misunderstandings. The "generation" here comes from the reader, not the teacher. The National Reading Panel noted that question generation had the strongest scientific support of any of the reading strategies they studied, and "may also best be used as a part of a multiple strategy instruction program" (National Institute of Child Health and Human Development, 2000, p. 8). Question generation is also useful for solving problems that are encountered in the text. These clarifications can occur at a number of levels, from the word to the idea. Effective readers notice when there is a problem with a word or idea and apply strategies to correct the error. Pressley points out that "[i]n doing so, comprehension in general should be improved, for much more of the text will be correctly decoded" (2000, p. 552).

Did you notice that when Nancy had a question, her first response was to talk to others? Questions and discussions go hand-in-hand, and this can be a great starting point for getting students more comfortable with the habit of questioning. One of our teacher friends, Aida Allen, loves to have students talk about their interests and understandings using divergent questions. This type of question allows students to think independently, creatively, and critically. The question starters Ms. Allen uses include:

- Imagine . . .
- Suppose . . .
- Predict . . .
- How might . . .
- Can you create . . .
- What are some of the possible consequences . . .
- What if . . .

Post these starters in a visible place in the classroom. Challenge yourself, and your students, to use them to foster thoughtful discussions, which is how they are used in reciprocal teaching groups.

We know children are great at asking questions: When's recess? How much longer till we get there? Will this be on the test? We also know they have the capacity to generate questions while they are reading. We think the reason that many students don't ask questions during reading is because they don't know how or when. A few of our favorite activities that begin to foster the habit of asking questions during reading include ReQuest, QAR, and QtA. We've used each of these approaches to help students learn to ask better questions.

Request

ReQuest (Manzo, 1969) is a useful questioning technique designed to help students formulate questions and answers based on a text passage. This procedure also builds background knowledge and vocabulary through discussions and helps readers develop predictions about their reading. The ReQuest technique is fairly simple to use, once students have been taught how. Students, in pairs, read a piece of text individually, stopping periodically to discuss the text. One student reads to identify questions to ask and the other reads to predict questions that might be asked and to think about possible answers.

We recently observed a ReQuest conversation between Bart and Heather. They were reading an article about trans fat and stopped several times to discuss the information from the text. At one point, Heather asked a number of questions, including:

- So what is trans fat?
- Can all foods be trans fat free?
- Why did New York City ban trans fat in restaurants?

The discussion that Bart and Heather had about these questions required that they return to the text, discuss possible answers, and negotiate meaning (or sense making) together. Had they not done so, we're not convinced that these two students would understand this important information about their health.

Question–Answer Relationships

The question–answer relationship (QAR) strategy describes four types of questions: right there, think and search, author and you, and on your own (Raphael, Highfield, & Au, 2006). QAR allows students to move beyond literal, recall questions and think about a number of text-explicit and text-implicit ways of thinking about their readings. Students can be taught these four question types and then begin to use them in their own discussions. For example, during a third-grade class discussion about the ways in which physical geography, including climate, influenced how the local Indian nations adapted to their natural environment, students wrote questions that they had and how they could answer them. In groups of four, they determined where they might be able to find the answers to the questions they had. Listening in on the conversation provides a glimpse about students' understanding of the role that questioning plays in reading.

At one point David read one of the questions and said, "You can't find that in a book, you have to think about that on your own." He was referring to the fact that the question asked about the climate that a person favored and why "you" lived where you do. At another point in the conversation, Mariah read one of the questions and said, "I bet we can find this in a book" and went to get *North American Indian*, an Eyewitness (2005) book that contains a great deal of information. And sure enough, Mariah found the answer to the question on a specific page of the book.

With practice, students learn that the four types of questions are useful in predicting where answers can be found. As great readers, students know to reread when they encounter *right there* or *think and search* questions. They also know that they should consider their own perspectives and other things they've read when they encounter *author and you* and *on your own* questions.

Question the Author

Questioning the author (QtA) is a text-based strategy that invites the reader to interact with the information and build meaning from the content by analyzing the author's purpose (Beck, McKeown, Hamilton, & Kucan, 1997). We often find that one of the reasons students don't question the text is because they don't view reading as a transactional activity. Using QtA, we can teach them to imagine that the author of the text is sitting next to them, and they can ask him or her questions. Young readers find this concept liberating, since they may not have previously thought about the person behind the words. The questions in QtA are meant to serve as discussion prompts that invite students to develop ideas rather than restate information directly from the text. These questions require that students take responsibility for their thinking and for constructing understanding.

During their whole-class discussion about *Because of Winn-Dixie* (DiCamillo, 2000) that the teacher was reading aloud, students used QtA to engage in a discussion about the book. The conversation started when Sitha asked, "What is the author trying to say, by making us see that Opal is very sad about her mom?" After several minutes of discussion in which students analyzed the author's message, Randi changed the subject with the question, "Why did the author tell us about the librarian fighting off a bear with a book? What does that have to do with the story?" Again, we are struck with the engagement and critical thinking displayed by students who know how to ask a really good question.

We're reminded of a poster that Ms. Allen has hanging in her room. On it, a Chinese proverb reminds students of the importance of asking questions. It reads: *"He who asks a question is a fool for five minutes; he who does not ask a question remains a fool forever."*

Clarifying

First and foremost, clarifying encourages students to monitor their own comprehension. This is one of the distinguishing differences between good and great readers. Poor readers give up when the going gets tough. Good readers may plod through the text, hoping it will make sense when they get to the end. Great readers, on the other hand, monitor their comprehension as they are reading, and apply fix-up strategies when they lose the meaning. In other words, great readers understand when their reading is problematic and when they should become strategic.

Of course, losing the meaning happens to us all. Nancy likes to read late at night before going to sleep. She knows that because she's tired, she might easily lose focus, reading the words but not thinking about what she just read. How often does that happen to you? Her recall might be reduced as a result, and she pays attention to her understanding to make sure that this doesn't happen. When she nods off a bit, Nancy likes to reread to make sure that she doesn't miss anything important. There are other ways to clarify, but rereading is a good one. If rereading doesn't help, she knows it's time to turn off the light and go to sleep. Nancy's students love when she shares this story with them and acts out the nodding off part. This funny story provides a memorable way to show our students that all readers clarify. Of course, it also helps to show our love of reading.

Readers need to learn to monitor their comprehension, their attention to the reading, and to notice when they're confused or not paying attention. Sometimes readers become confused by a word. Other times, they're confused by an idea. For example, Doug was reading information about which new TV to buy—high definition, plasma, etc. Finding websites about this is easy. Reading them isn't. Here's a sample:

> MPEG-2 is most commonly used as the compression code for digital HDTV broadcasts. Although MPEG-2 supports up to 4:2:2 YCbCr chroma subsampling and 10-bit quantization, HD broadcasts use 4:2:0 and 8-bit quantization to save bandwidth.

Huh? Was that your reaction? After he read these lines, Doug knew he was confused. But the strategy of rereading didn't help. Is it vocabulary that gets in the way? Are the ideas unclear? Is Doug's background knowledge insufficient to understand the text? The answer to all of these questions is yes. The important thing is that Doug knew this passage didn't make sense to him and found help. That's what we have to have our students do—notice. Of course, we have to teach them what to do once they notice, but the first step is to notice. The next day, Doug brought this passage into his classroom, and read it aloud to his students. He modeled the confusion he experienced as he read these words. Sharing our authentic struggles to make sense of complex text is one of the best ways to help our students understand how to notice.

Once you notice the confusion, your next step is to identify the cause. One cause of confusion is unfamiliar words. When students realize that the words are confusing, we teach them that the inside/outside perspective helps. Over time, students learn that they can look for meanings of words inside the word by using morphology, affixes, and cognates. For example, when Kelli came across the word *microcosm* in the sentence, "Our town is a microcosm of life in the United States," she knew that *micro-* meant small. She also knew *cosmic* and *cosmopolitan* related to the world and made an educated guess that microcosm was a small world. Her meaning fit in the sentence and helped her verify her understanding of the text.

In addition, students can go outside the word to figure it out. This requires that they use context clues, syntax, and grammar structures to determine what the word means. Thankfully, many writers are considerate of their readers. When they use difficult or unfamiliar terms, they often embed a definition or use an analogy to help the reader. Consider the following sentence describing an experience diving: "In between clearing flooded masks or removing our air supplies, we would gesticulate wildly, flapping our hands to point out the giant barracuda hovering nearby, its ugly jaws snapping." In this case, students can go outside the word to figure out what *gesticulate* means.

Clarifying ideas is a bit more complex, because confusing ideas typically require that students build their background knowledge. When Adam comes to a confusing idea in something he's reading, he usually puts that reading aside and reads related texts to build his understanding. For example, when Adam was first developing a new unit on the Middle Ages for his sixth-grade class, he picked up a college textbook on the art of the time period at a used bookstore. However, he quickly realized this text wasn't making much sense to him because he didn't possess enough background knowledge on medieval life. He decided it would make sense to read some books that provided an overview of the time period before he delved back into the artwork. Once Adam clarified his understanding of the feudal system and monastic life, he was ready to tackle the more complex art book.

Reading more books isn't always the answer. Another strategy Adam uses to clarify confusing ideas is to talk to people. In this case, Adam heeded the advice of his own sixth-grade teacher, whose mantra was to "talk it out," in this case, with an experienced colleague. Discussion is one of the ways we all learn and clarify. Our students need to do the same; they need to read widely so that they have systems for building background knowledge and they need to be in classrooms where talking is encouraged and facilitated. Seeking clarification should be seen as a strength, not a weakness. Great readers know this and discuss their ideas with others while they search for meaning. We frequently ask our students to simply "turn and talk" during a lesson. Those brief clarifying conversations help to deepen their understanding and foster the habit of maintaining an internal dialogue to seek meaning.

Making Predictions

Making predictions is one of the most complex tasks we ask students to perform. Predictions are not wild guesses, rather sophisticated estimations based on a complex understanding of the text and the world. Like other systems for making sense of text, students need a great deal of modeling to become effective and efficient predictors. They also need huge stores of background knowledge on which they can draw. This, of course, requires that they read a lot. You might be tired of us saying this, but one of the most important things we can do for our students is to get them reading and reading a lot!

Contrary to what some believe, predicting is not "just for kids," but is a complex process and one that requires a great deal of practice. As Wolsey and Fisher (2008) note, predicting is part of human history and has served us well. For example, early humans used prediction skills for determining where they might find food supplies. Early humans also predicted danger from certain animals and identified places that would keep them safe at night. Humans regularly assess dangers relative to their personal safety using predictions. Even though Anthony could make predictions about the world around him (e.g., when it was going to rain, when it was safe to cross the street, what the consequences of not doing his math homework might be), he did not apply this knowledge to his reading.

For students to learn to predict, we need to focus them on the process of predicting and not simply on making a prediction. By process, we mean the factors that readers take into consideration to make a prediction. When students make predictions, they need to consider:

- What will the text be about?
- What clues do the title and illustrations provide?
- What will happen early versus later in the text?
- What are different possible outcomes?

Once they have made their initial predictions, students should be able to answer:

- What are you basing your predictions on?
- Are you equally confident that all of your predictions about the text will come true?
- What evidence do you expect that the author will provide?

We fear that too many students get the wrong notion about predicting, and school is to blame. Too often, young readers come away with the false impression that predicting is something that happens only *before* the reading. You have probably read thrillers like *The Da Vinci Code* (Brown, 2003) or *The Spy Who Came*

John Graham

in From the Cold (LaCarre, 1964). Chances are good that you didn't make a prediction at the very beginning and then doggedly held on to that idea despite mounting evidence to the contrary. Instead, you kept revising your initial predictions, drawing on your background knowledge of the genre. You questioned whether each new development was a clue or a canard, foreshadowing or merely a red herring. Likewise, as they read, our students should consider:

- Are your predictions confirmed or disconfirmed?
- Do you need to revise your predictions based on what you have read?
- Why are you altering your prediction?

And finally, after reading, students need to be pushed to metacognitive levels of understanding predicting by considering:

- How did the process of making and revisiting predictions help you to understand the text?
- What helped you make and revise predictions (vocabulary, background knowledge, literary devices, text structure, point of view)?

Source: Cover from *The Invention of Hugo Cabret* by Brian Selznick. Copyright © 2007 by Brian Selznick. Reprinted by permission of Scholastic Inc.

Although these questions can be easily turned into a worksheet (which we don't advise), their power is in their repeated use. Through ongoing modeling and prompting during whole-group, small-group, and individual discussions, students begin to think in these ways, making predictions before they read, looking for confirming or disproving evidence, revising predictions as they read, and reflecting on their predictions when they have finished reading. As we travel around our classrooms, we ask students questions like these to jumpstart their thinking, but not always.

As students advance, our instruction on predicting goes deeper. Although we still encourage students to make predictions based on the cover or the title, we also teach students to use their knowledge of text structures and text features to make predictions. For example, once a student recognizes that a book about tornadoes is organized by cause and effect, she might predict that she'll learn what causes tornadoes to form. If a student is reading a book about exploration and sees a map that shows the route of an explorer, he can predict he will read about when and where the explorer traveled.

All this talk about predictions causes us to remember Janet who answered, "How should I know?" the first time we asked her to make a prediction about a book. Janet didn't have much experience reading for her own reasons. She "read" what she was assigned and answered questions dutifully. However, she lacked the experience of being deeply engaged with a book. Thus, the curiosity that burns inside a reader who has just got to find out if he's right had never occurred for her. With a lot of modeling and practice using books that Janet was interested in, she began making predictions on her own. It's important to note that these early attempts were not very sophisticated and tended to rely on obvious clues. But over time, Janet became a consumer of books, as well as a critic. She evaluated books, predicting whether or not they would inform or entertain her, and she could explain why. The last time we saw Janet, she was in the classroom library holding two different books. When asked about them, she said, "I'm deciding which I want to read. I predict that they'll both be good. I estimate that I can read this one faster, but that I might be more focused with this one. Obviously they're both about orphans, but with a twist. I'm thinking that I'll choose *The Invention of Hugo Cabret* (Selznick, 2007) because I want to see if I'm right about his real identity."

MOVING FROM GOOD TO GREAT

The following example comes from Anthony two years after we first met him. Anthony had a sudden and profound interest in parasitic fungi in insects. Apparently he was watching *Plant Earth* on the Discovery Channel and simply had to know more about this. If you are like us and don't know a lot about the topic, then it helps to know that there are a number of parasitic fungi that manipulate their host insect to increase their own chances of reproducing. The results are pretty spectacular, in a stomach-churning kind of way (think of the scene in the movie *Alien*). It's a rather bizarre part of the animal kingdom, and one that Anthony wanted to know more about. The section of text under investigation at the time follows:

> The spores of the fungus attach themselves to the external surface of the ant, where they germinate. They then enter the ant's body through the tracheae (the tubes through which insects breathe), via holes in the exoskeleton called spiracles. Fine fungal filaments called mycelia then start to grow inside the ant's body cavity, absorbing the host's soft tissues but avoiding its vital organs

We overhead Anthony talking with Jeremiah about this section of text on the website they were reading. As you'll see, Anthony moved well beyond the "word caller" stage and was engaged in an authentic discussion using skills and strategies.

Anthony: Okay, so this is how it is. The fungus starts on the outside and then gets in the bug. But it doesn't kill it. It takes over like . . .

Jeremiah: Crazy. The fungus knows not to hurt the heart or lungs or stuff. I don't know what it means, body cavity. Like a tooth the body gets rotten?

Anthony: Open a new window and look it up. [opens a browser window]

Jeremiah: Oh, no way, it gets into the body fluid part.

Anthony: Sick. See that's how it doesn't kill the insect. It's in between the skin and organs, getting bigger. I wonder how come the ant can't get rid of it.

Jeremiah: Maybe it doesn't know, like when you get a cold at first you don't know. But the cold doesn't kill you, but still, you don't know at first.

Anthony: But on the show, the bug did get killed. I think it will get killed. And the other ones will get killed too, if they don't get away.

Jeremiah: That's messed up. Do you think humans can get this? Do those funguses get into us?

While you might argue that the text Anthony and Jeremiah selected might be a bit hard for them, they were able to understand a great deal about the natural world from reading and talking. Importantly, they used both skills and strategies to make sense of the text. What they didn't do is stop their investigation and discussion to say something as absurd as, "Now I'd like to make a prediction." Instead, summarizing, questioning, clarifying, and predicting were natural parts of their search for understanding. Their discussion demanded that they use these approaches to learn from the text. Keep this goal in mind as you teach each of these strategies. Ultimately, we want our readers to use these strategies flexibly and interchangeably. To put this in more technical language, the Report of the National Reading Panel says, ". . . multiple strategy instruction that is flexible as to which strategies are used and when they are taught over the course of a reading session provides a natural basis on which teachers and readers can interact over text" (National Institute of Child Health and Human Development, 2000, p. 9).

As noted at the beginning of this chapter, we used the elements of reciprocal teaching as an organizer to describe the habits employed by effective readers to comprehend text. As you have noticed in your own reading, you draw upon these techniques unconsciously most of the time (a habit), and deliberately at others when the text has been particularly challenging (a strategy). Moving readers from good to great as they make sense of text requires instructing them on how these sense-making techniques fall together. Reciprocal teaching is an ideal method for accomplishing this.

Lori Oczkus (2003) has done a great job in describing a method for introducing reciprocal teaching first through a series of whole-class lessons, each focusing on just one of the elements. As students become more comfortable with say, summarizing, she introduces them to a new strategy. She says that a major goal during these whole-class lessons is "to establish a common language for using reciprocal teaching strategies" that can then be shifted to small-group teacher-guided sessions (p. 32).

The guided lesson groups are composed of four students, each with a role as a summarizer, questioner, clarifier, or predictor, and the teacher, who is there to guide the conversation and model as needed. These reciprocal teaching groups are still pretty structured, because students are still working at the level of strategy acquisition. Over time, and with coaching from the teacher, these strategies begin to take on the qualities of habits, as readers become more fluent in engaging in these cognitive processes.

Oczkus goes on to describe her move to literature circle discussions, where readers who have been equipped with these strategies can enter into conversations that are more fluid and less staged than previous sessions. Students still have roles, but over time these tend to drop by the wayside as readers enter into authentic discourse about a book. Harvey Daniels (2006), the originator of literature circles, has written of the overuse of roles that lead to "mechanical discussions," which interfere with the natural ebb and flow of meaningful conversations (p. 11). From our experience, the teacher who is afraid to let go of the structured nature of reciprocal teaching after students have grown more competent is often the one unintentionally preventing students from moving from good to great.

So how do you know they're ready? The short answer is that you don't always "know." However, the checklist below is a good starting point for assessing students' movement from strategy to habit.

Does the student:

Summarize and Synthesize

- Pause during reading to take brief notes?
- Explain how to use a text feature, such as headings, to summarize?
- Distinguish between important and unimportant ideas?

Ask Questions

- Ask *Who? What? Where?* and *When?* questions when reading?
- Ask *Why?* questions or make *I wonder* statements when reading?
- Formulate text-implicit questions and use text clues and prior knowledge and experience to answer those questions?
- Identify the author's purpose based on questions he or she would like to ask the author?

Clarify

- Read on to find the meaning of unfamiliar words?
- Look for context clues to figure out unfamiliar words?
- Stop and reread to understand unfamiliar concepts?
- Resolve confusions by discussing them with a partner?
- Consult other books for clarification?

Predict

- Make predictions that are relevant to the text?
- Continue to revise predictions during reading?
- Use prior knowledge to make predictions?
- Use text structure and/or text features to make predictions?

Professional Development

1. Let students see the authentic questions that your colleagues are asking. For example, if you hold faculty meetings in the school library, keep the questions you raise (appropriate ones of course) on display for students to use.
2. Designate a public place in your school, perhaps near the front entrance, to display a bulletin board titled, "Our Burning Questions: Can You Help?" Leave out index cards, and invite community members (fellow students, parents, etc.) to share possible answers.

3. As adults we sometimes forget how summarizing can help us make sense of text. Use paired reading at faculty meetings to discuss new policies or professional articles. One partner reads a paragraph aloud, and the other partner summarizes what was read aloud. Then switch.

4. Make sure parents understand the range and complexity of predictions they can model when they read aloud. Feature making predictions the topic of one of your parent newsletters columns, and share some of the questions posed in this chapter.

References

Anderson, C. (2006). *The long tail: Why the future of business is selling less of more.* New York: Hyperion.

Armbruster, B. B., Anderson, T. H., & Ostertag, J. (1987). Does text structure/summarization instruction facilitate learning from expository text? *Reading Research Quarterly, 22,* 331–346.

Ballard, R. D. (1988). *Exploring the Titanic.* New York: Scholastic.

Beck, I., McKeown, M., Hamilton, R., & Kucan, L. (1997). *Questioning the author: An approach for enhancing student engagement with text.* Newark, DE: International Reading Association.

Brown, D. (2003). *The Da Vinci code.* New York: Doubleday.

Daniels, H. (2006). What's the next big thing in literature circles? *Voices From the Middle, 13*(4), 10–15.

DiCamillo, K. (2000). *Because of Winn-Dixie.* New York: Candlewick.

Eyewitness. (2005). *North American Indian.* New York: DK Publishing.

Graff, G., & Birkenstein, C. (2006). *They say/I say: The moves that matter in academic writing.* New York: W. W. Norton & Company.

Harvey, S. (1998). *Nonfiction matters: Reading, writing, and research in grades 3–8.* York, ME: Stenhouse.

Hatkoff, I., Hatkoff, C., & Kahumbu, P. (2006). *Owen & Mzee: The true story of a remarkable friendship.* New York: Scholastic.

LaCarre, J. (1964). *The spy who came in from the cold.* New York: Coward-McCann.

Manzo, A. V. (1969). ReQuest procedure. *Journal of Reading, 13,* 123–126.

Marzano, R., Pickering, D., & Pollock, J. (2001). *Classroom instruction that works: Research-based strategies for increasing student achievement.* Alexandria, VA: Association for Supervision and Curriculum Development.

National Institute of Child Health and Human Development. (2000). *Report of the National Reading Panel. Teaching children to read: An evidence-based assessment of the scientific research literature on reading and its implications for reading instruction: Reports of the subgroups: Comprehension* (NIH Publication No. 00-4754). Washington, DC: U.S. Government Printing Office.

Oczkus, L. D. (2003). *Reciprocal teaching at work: Strategies for improving reading comprehension.* Newark, DE: International Reading Association.

Palincsar, A. S., & Brown, A. (1984). Reciprocal teaching of comprehension-fostering and comprehension monitoring activities. *Cognition and Instruction, 1*(2), 117–175.

Palincsar, A. S., & Klenk, L. (1991). Dialogues promoting reading comprehension. In B. Means, C. Chelemer, & M. S. Knapp (Eds.), *Teaching advanced skills to at-risk students* (pp. 112–140). San Francisco: Jossey-Bass.

Paris, S. G., Wasik, B. A., & Turner, J. C. (1991). The development of strategic readers. In R. Barr, M. L. Kamil, P. Mosenthal, & P. D. Pearson (Eds.), *Handbook of reading research* (Vol. II, pp. 609–640). Mahwah, NJ: Lawrence A. Erlbaum.

Pressley, M. (2000). What should comprehension instruction be the instruction of? In M. L. Kamil, P. B. Moenthal, P. D. Pearson, & R. Barr (Eds.), *Handbook of reading research* (Vol. III, pp. 545–562). Mahwah, NJ: Lawrence A. Erlbaum.

Raphael, T. E., Highfield, K., & Au, K. H. (2006). *QAR now: A powerful and practical framework that develops comprehension and higher-level thinking in all students.* New York: Scholastic.

Selznick, B. (2007). *The invention of Hugo Cabret.* New York: Scholastic.

Spinelli, J. (1999). *Maniac Magee.* New York: Little, Brown Young Readers.

Wolsey, T. D., & Fisher, D. (2008). *Learning to predict and predicting to learn.* Upper Saddle River, NJ: Merrill Prentice Hall.

CHAPTER 4

Great Readers Use What They Know

It's unlikely that anyone would argue that great readers use what they know. However, using the *right* knowledge is trickier. Sometimes applying what one knows to a reading is helpful and other times it's not. Regardless of the helpfulness, it is a fact that readers *will* use what they already know. We can't stop them. Consider Tyler, a fourth-grader who loves turtles. It seems that he knows all there is to know about turtles and constantly reads about them, draws them, and writes reports about them. (He also convinced his teacher, Adam, to get a class turtle. Luckily for Adam, Tyler doesn't mind cleaning the tank.) His ability to read complex texts well above his assessed reading level is apparent when he consults a 416-page book called *Turtles of the World* (Bonin, Devaux, & Dupré, 2006). Of course, there are words he doesn't know and the sentence structure can get thorny. However, his knowledge of the subject facilitates his reading of this challenging book. It's easy to see that his ability to use what he knows helps him understand what he reads.

We call this background knowledge. It's been written about extensively; background knowledge plays a crucial role in reading achievement. We carry this background knowledge with us wherever we go. Doug can't read something about rural life without thinking about raising pigs, caring for his horse, and the pressure on the family to make enough money. (If you are curious, Doug grew up in Alpine, California.) It's not like any of us, or any of your readers, can set this knowledge aside while reading. It's also not possible to instantly create background knowledge where there isn't any. We've seen the puzzled faces when a second-grade teacher asks her inner-city class to complete the "K" section of a K-W-L chart on a 4H Fair—it's too removed from the experiences of many of these young children.

While there are all kinds of positive impacts from having background knowledge, it's crucial to notice when this knowledge is not helpful. When a substitute in Tyler's class tried to read a fable about the hare and the tortoise, Tyler couldn't help himself. He tried to educate the substitute about the difference between tortoises and turtles and what they could really do. As Tyler tried to explain, "No, a tortoise wouldn't do that. He doesn't want to run. When it's hot outside, he finds shade to stay cool." Tyler's background knowledge wasn't much help and, in fact, blocked his understanding of the fable. While he knew a lot about tortoises, he lacked background knowledge in fables as a genre.

HELPING STUDENTS USE WHAT THEY KNOW

Although evident to great readers, this habit isn't well developed in many classrooms, perhaps because it's easier said than done. Instead of figuring out what students know and building from there, too often students are assigned books they aren't interested in. Tradition sometimes plays a role, such as the notion that all third-graders must read *Charlotte's Web* (White, 1952). Now this book is beloved by many, but it can't be assumed that it resonates with every child. Too often, students are assigned to read books they don't care about, can't read, or don't have the background knowledge to understand. You'd have to set aside lots of time for building background if you wanted to read *Charlotte's Web* to inner-city students. It seems that as educators we know about the importance of interest as it relates to motivation, but overlook student interest as insight into the background knowledge they possess. After all, it is unlikely that you are interested in a topic for which you possess no knowledge.

Miriam really taught us this. As a third-grader, Miriam wanted to please her teacher more than anything else. Miriam interpreted this to mean that she should read every book that the teacher recommended. She would take a book and slog her way through it. When Nancy realized this, she had a conversation with her about what she likes, what she knows about, and what she wants to know more about. It turns out that Miriam is fascinated by the Wild West, cowboys, and all things western. Since then, Nancy's been on the lookout for good titles for her to read. She can still make recommendations, but these can be informed by the background knowledge Miriam possesses. As a result of our experiences with Miriam and other students like her, we have developed or adopted a few interest inventories that we use with students to determine what they know and are interested in, as you saw in Chapter 2. Not only do the results of interest inventories provide ways to motivate students, they also give us a glimpse of their background knowledge. Books like these give Miriam opportunities to move from a good reader to a great one, as she incorporates her background knowledge into her reading.

Of course, at times we all have to read things on topics that are unfamiliar to us. At those times, we revert and become strategic readers. In doing so, we purposefully use specific strategies that we have been taught. These might include making a list of things you already know, talking with others about the topic, reading related sources to figure out the harder reading, and so on.

In the next section, we'll describe four aspects to building the habit of using what you know. These habits emphasize marshalling the skills and strategies one already possesses. They include:

1. Activating Background Knowledge
2. Making Connections
3. Building Vocabulary and Concept Knowledge
4. Inferencing

Hope Madden/Merril

Activating Background Knowledge

Great readers first activate their background knowledge by previewing the text. When Nancy saw the cover of *Left for Dead: A Young Man's Search for Justice for the USS Indianapolis* (Nelson, 2003), she immediately began cataloging what she knew about the topic. She knew a bit about the story of the Navy cruiser that was torpedoed during WWII. The picture of the shark on the cover reminded her that she knew that some of the men who survived the blast were attacked by sharks during the four days they floated in the water. She had also been to Indianapolis, Indiana, many times during her childhood, but dismissed that information right away because she figured this book didn't have anything to do with the city. She read the back cover and flipped through the photographs on the glossy pages of the book. She skimmed the preface written by Hunter Scott, the 11-year-old boy whose history fair project on the tragedy led to a reopening of the case in 1999. How could a kid do that? She was sold! She knew that she (and some of her students) would be gripped by this book.

That's what we want all readers to be able to do. When they pick up a text, we want them to activate their mental search engine, searching for information that will help them construct meaning before they read. We also want them to weed out what they don't need. We also hoped that you noticed how Nancy's example involves making predictions, which we discussed in the last chapter, but goes one step further. Students also need to begin building a schema for what they will read. We explain to our students that a schema is a framework, and ask them to think of examples of structural frames that support. In no time they have brainstormed a list: the wooden frame of a house, the veins of a leaf, the skeleton. After this activity, each time we begin a read-aloud we set aside a few minutes to build our "schema," it's one of those technical terms our kids love to say aloud.

At times Doug uses realia to demonstrate how the brain organizes clusters of information into a mental set (schema). Using an unassembled cardboard file box purchased at an office supply store, he begins by labeling the flat box "Vegetables" and shows the students that merely piling a lot of vegetables on top of the cardboard won't make for reliable storage. As he talks about the characteristics of vegetables, he starts assembling the box. On each side he writes a characteristic: Edible Plant Part, Leaves, Roots, and Flower. He then sorts vegetables from bread items to visually demonstrate how a schema helps us store information in a place it can be found, and where new ideas can be added. He reminds them that labeling the box is akin to using one's background knowledge because we begin building that framework using the information we already possess. Once we have a framework, or schema, we can add lots of new knowledge. Demonstrations and think-alouds such as these are the backbone of our instruction.

Using Think-alouds

Jeff Wilhelm (2001) helped us further our understanding of how student think-alouds could be used by readers to activate their background knowledge as they "hear how others sleuth out and make sense of all these text clues" (p. 19). We like that notion of being a *sleuth*, because it represents an active and deliberate process. First, we model our own think-aloud, since many of our students don't understand what it means "to think aloud." Please see Figure 4.1 for a sample teacher think-aloud on *Ox-Cart Man* (Hall, 1984). For some students, it helps if we invite them to "riff on a book" (as DeJuan has described it) to show us how they construct a preliminary schema. *Riff* is another word that resonates with many of our students. It's fascinating to watch, like witnessing time-lapsed photography of a flower blossom opening. If you know to look for it, and know how to look, a new perspective is revealed.

Source: From *Ox-Cart Man*, by Donald Hall. Illustration done by Barbara Cooney. Copyright © 1979 Penguin Group. Reprinted with permission.

Using Text Features

In addition to teacher and student think-alouds, we teach students to use the text features of the book to develop questions about what they

FIGURE 4.1 Sample Think-aloud

> The title of this book is *Ox-Cart Man.* I don't know much about ox carts, but I do know about horse carts. I guess oxen pull carts, just the way horses do. As I look at the cover illustration, I think this is about a man who owns an ox that pulls his cart. I know an ox is a strong work animal. I've also heard the expression strong as an ox. This man looks like he lived long ago. His clothes look like the kind people wore 200 years ago. I know that people so long ago didn't have cars and used carts pulled by animals to travel. Now that I am thinking about what I already know, I feel more ready to start reading this book.

don't know. We'll talk more about text features in Chapter 6, but briefly text features include title, headings, diagrams, illustrations, and photographs. This activity allows them to figure out where the gaps are in their knowledge, so they can decide whether this is the book they need. Generating questions that link background knowledge to text features also prepares them for what the author is likely to tell them over the course of the book. Nancy sits with her young students and asks them to do a "picture walk" of their own before beginning a new informational book. They place self-sticking notes of different colors on illustrations to denote what they know (green), what looks completely new (red), and what's got them curious (yellow). A book with a combination of all three colors indicates that it is a good choice as it contains information that is familiar as well as information to learn.

Students need to be purposeful about building their background knowledge, because complex texts sometimes require another resource. Doug asks his students to pair new books with resource materials. They don't need to retrieve the dictionary or encyclopedia and put it in their desk, but he does want them to make a note of where they might find more information to clarify difficult concepts. His students call them "Unstuck-y Notes" and they affix them to the inside cover of the book. They write the names of useful resources in the classroom that they can turn to, and leave the notes there for future readers. A reminder to look at the *Eyewitness American Revolution* book (Murray, 2005) is helpful when reading *Johnny Tremain* (Forbes, 1998), and causes the reader to consider in advance where he or she might turn for more information. Just like an experienced detective who's always on the lookout for clues, we want our sleuths to pay attention to what they know and to what they don't know yet.

Making Connections

Activating background knowledge slides elegantly into making connections. We don't spend a lot of time differentiating the two (although we are discussing them separately here). In *Mosaic of Thought*, Ellin Keene and Susan Zimmerman (2007) identify three types of connections.

- Text-to-Self
- Text-to-Text
- Text-to-World

We spend some time during the school year discussing these different types of connections but we don't hang posters around the room with this language because over time it fossilizes our students' thinking. One year, our students made mention of lots of connections to be made:

- Music
- Paintings and photographs
- Places visited
- Other languages students know
- Problems students have solved
- History and science
- Beliefs and values
- Feelings experienced
- Ideas
- Conversations with other people
- Things written down
- Stuff thought of later

Most of these can be sorted into text-to-self/text/world, but our goal is to expand their connections, not continually reduce them to a few categories. We are not aiming to have lots of children saying things like, "I'd like to make a text-to-world connection," because this is ultimately artificial. Imagine the grimaces that would occur at your next adult book club gathering if someone said such a thing. Nancy knew it had gone too far when Robert told her, "I have a text-to-text connection with an episode of *SpongeBob SquarePants*."

Don't misunderstand—we believe the language Keene and Zimmermann (2007) introduced to us has been invaluable in giving teachers the vocabulary for making connections explicit. But keep in mind that when they speak of a "mosaic of thought," they metaphorically describe how strategies fit together to fashion a meaningful whole. Temporarily deconstructing strategies for initial learning is useful, but they should be assimilated as soon as possible with other skills. A deconstructed mosaic, after all, is just a pile of tiles.

In truth, those connections we make are continual and come at odd moments. Therefore, we spend time asking our students to share connections with one another, so they can hear for themselves that each reader's connections are as unique as a fingerprint. We model our own connections for them, so that they can see the ways we make decisions related to connections. During guided instruction, we allot time for sharing these connections as a group. We invite students to think about what the text reminded them of, and to discuss the similarities and differences between their musings. The emphasis is less on filling out worksheets of forced connections, and more on the conversation that comes when readers marvel at the ways their thinking is analogous and unique all at once. We like to share these labels with students, because we want them to understand the range of connections they might make.

Nancy sat down with first-grade student Jocelyn to listen in on the types of connections she was making as she read. Jocelyn is familiar with thinking aloud, and as she read the informational picture book *Houses and Homes* (Morris, 1995), she seemed to stall on making connections with the photographs of homes that were unfamiliar to her. Nancy decided to revisit the concept of connections with her, using a metacognitive questioning grid (see Figure 4.2 at the end of this chapter) she keeps for reference in her conferring binder. She asked Jocelyn to think about what she already knew about connections, who replied, "They're ideas you have when you read, like for stuff you already know." Nancy then asked Jocelyn to think about the topic of the book and to predict the kinds of connections a person reading the book might make. The two of them discussed personal connections ("We all live in a house," Jocelyn offered), and noted differences between her house and the ones in the book ("Where do they put the kitchen?" she wondered). Nancy then took Jocelyn back to the beginning of the book and the two of them thought aloud together, with Nancy modeling the kinds of connections she anticipated Jocelyn could make. Jocelyn elaborated on the connections and even initiated a few of her own. Based on this conversation, Nancy noted that Jocelyn was gaining awareness of connections as a part of her reading, but that these connections were not automatic. Nancy jotted down in Jocelyn's file that she needed more practice with this habit.

Building Vocabulary and Concept Knowledge

In this section, we are purposefully linking two large topics together because we feel that they can't be discussed separately. It reminds us of the fable of the elephant and the seven blind men, none of whom could grasp the concept of the whole because they could only discern the parts. Research tells us that vocabulary is the best predictor of knowledge, far better than an IQ score (Farley & Elmore, 1992). Vocabulary and reading comprehension are closely linked because of the relationship between words and conceptual knowledge (Beck, Perfetti, & McKeown, 1982). Concept knowledge is an understanding of ideas, whereas words are labels for these ideas.

Students learn vocabulary in a variety of ways, including within the context of the reading itself. However, their ability to be able to glean contextual understanding from the reading requires active teaching. This happens through direct instruction (Stahl, 1983) and application of intentional strategies to figure out the meaning of the words (Blachowicz & Fisher, 2000).

A direct instruction approach to vocabulary involves providing definitional lessons about words that are essential for understanding a piece of text. We use several research-based techniques to provide direct instruction on vocabulary—conceptual word sorts, word derivations, affixes, and using reference materials like dictionaries (Brassell & Flood, 2004). Children benefit from explicit and definitional teaching in the technical vocabulary they will encounter in a reading—*photosynthesis*, *westward expansion*, and *multiplication*—in order to understand a text in which they will encounter such words (Beck et al., 1982).

Vocabulary Role-Play

Students also benefit from experiences that allow them to internalize new vocabulary so that they can call upon a definition of a word when they need it in reading. Vocabulary role-play (Frey & Fisher, 2007) is a popular activity in our classes when we need students to absorb lots of technical words quickly. Sentence strips are prepared with the words we have been studying, and students take turns coming to the front of the class. The word is held over the child's head so that the entire class, but not our volunteer, can see it. The job of the class is to pantomime the word in an effort for the student to guess the term. You haven't lived until you've seen a class of fourth-graders acting out the word *denominator* by crouching under their desks, while others stood on the desks to represent *numerator*. It's even more interesting to explain what it was they were doing to the principal who happened to walk by at that moment.

Inside/Outside Words

In addition to learning specific words they will encounter in a text, students also need to learn how to structurally and contextually figure out unfamiliar words. James Baumann and his colleagues have described the utility of a combined approach that includes morphemic instruction to understand word parts such as affixes and roots, coupled with contextual instruction to show students how to look around a word to find the meaning (Baumann et al., 2002). When you think about it, it makes quite a bit of sense. Consider a time when you've encountered an unfamiliar word, like the one in the sentence below:

> The candidates' slanderous charges of one another's conduct during the campaign resulted in an *imbroglio* as the news media reported conflicting information.

In all likelihood, you used both approaches to figure out that *imbroglio* meant a "tangled mess":

- It reminded you of *embroilment* (morphemic).
- You used what you knew about slander, the news media, and conflicting reports to arrive at an approximation of the meaning (contextual).

However, the sentence could have been contextually impoverished as well. "No one expected the imbroglio that followed" is more difficult if you don't already know the word, and you may or may not have made the "embroilment" link without those other supporting clauses. When we're reading, we use all of these—definitional knowledge, morphemic analysis, and contextual clues—to make meaning. That's why it's so important that we not only "teach vocabulary," but that we also teach how we integrate the ways we use what we know to figure things out as we read. When we model our thinking and ask our students to explain theirs, we build habits that extend beyond a single lesson.

Doug models his thinking about unfamiliar words using an inside/outside strategy (Fisher & Frey, in press). When he comes to a cumbersome word like *cumbersome*, he tells his students,

> The first thing I'm going to do is to look inside the word. That means I need to break the word apart to see if I can figure out pieces of its meaning. I don't know what *cumber-* means, and that doesn't really sound familiar. *Cucumber*, that's about all I can think of. But it ends in *-some*, and that makes me think of *awesome*, something big. I don't know if that's right, so I have to try it out in the sentence. [He reads] "Antonio stumbled under the weight of his cumbersome load of pots and pans." Well, cucumber doesn't make any sense in that sentence, so I am ruling that out. I thought that *-some* at the end of that word might be something big, and that could work. But I can't be sure, so I am going to look outside the word, at this sentence,

and the ones around it. The next sentence reads, "Even though they were difficult to carry, he knew his family would be unable to survive in the mountains with these simple kitchen items." Yes, cumbersome does mean big, but it's more than that. There are clues outside the word that help me understand it. The author talks about the "weight" of the pots and pans, and in the next sentence he says they were "difficult to carry." I can put the inside and outside clues together to figure out that *cumbersome* means something that is big, heavy, and hard to carry.

That may seem like a lot of time spent on one word, but the teaching point has less to do with learning *cumbersome* than it does with learning a problem-solving method for building one's own vocabulary.

List-Group-Label

The goal of learning all this vocabulary is to use it in oral language, reading, and writing. That means promoting transfer of vocabulary skills across these dimensions of literacy. Hilda Taba (1967) developed the list-group-label approach when Nancy was in elementary school, and it is still useful with our learners today. This is an effective means for modeling how we link vocabulary and concepts to reading. We begin by inviting students to briefly scan the reading, focusing on titles and illustrations. For example, before reading *The Explorer's Handbook: How to Become an Intrepid Traveler* (Tolhurst, 1998), Doug asks his students to think about what they know about Vikings and begins listing their responses: They're fighters, they wear hats with horns on them, it's the name of a football team, and so on. He points out that they have activated their collective background knowledge and developed a list of vocabulary words associated with Vikings. He then asks them to work in partners to group the words and place them into labeled categories of their own creation, and then discuss their work with another pair. The class reconvenes, and Doug leads the discussion about the categories they have developed and sorts the associated terms. Doug then reminds them that these groupings should give them some ideas about the vocabulary and concepts they are likely to encounter in the reading. After they have completed the reading, they eliminate the vocabulary that did not appear (such as the Minnesota Vikings) and add new terms to the existing categories. In addition, they develop new categories, such as Famous Vikings, and add vocabulary terms like Eric the Red and Leif Erikson. This modeled lesson allows Doug to get his students using the vocabulary orally as they activate background knowledge and make connections. He doesn't do this for every reading, rather encourages them to do it in their minds.

Inferencing

Inferencing is among the most difficult of the reading comprehension strategies, as many teachers can attest. Students have labored for years under the decidedly unhelpful "read between the lines" cue with little success. That's unfortunate, since the ability to inference meanings not explicitly stated is a linchpin to comprehension (Collins, Brown, & Larkin, 1980). The challenge is that inferencing requires that the reader use what she knows to understand the unstated. For example, the

Doug Menuez/Getty Images, Inc. –Photodisc

sentence "The boy's lower lip began to quiver after he opened his last present" implies any of the following:

- He's sad and about to cry.
- He's upset because there are no more presents.
- He's upset because he didn't get what he really wanted.

One or more of these will probably be confirmed in the next few sentences, and it's possible that the author foreshadowed this event, perhaps mentioning the new skateboard he had been eyeing, or providing examples of his greediness. In any case, the reader has to bring a lot to the sentence in order to fully understand it.

Because many readers tend to infer only at the minimal level necessary (McKoon & Ratcliff, 1992), it is essential that the teacher create time and opportunity for students to infer at deeper levels (Kintsch, 2004).

We've known a number of students who have struggled with this process. It's not a surprise given the estimate that there can be "as many as 12 to 15 implicit inferences for every expressly mentioned statement" (Weaver & Kintsch, 1991, p. 235). Jacqueline, a first-grader, used to stare at other children when they read, rather than look at her own book. One day we asked her what she was doing, and she said, "I'm watching their heads." When we asked her to explain, she told us that she didn't understand how everyone else seemed to know what the characters were thinking when it "didn't say so in the book." At that moment we realized that Jacqueline hadn't yet figured out what others seemed to do so easily. She thought that looking at the heads of her peers might give her a clue about how they understand what they read.

We typically introduce inferencing by using something students are familiar with—comic strips. We invite students to talk about how they know what is occurring from one panel to the next, even if the picture doesn't show it. They will tell us that they "can just tell" and we explore this with them. We look at the visual vocabulary of the artist—like those horizontal lines that signal the speedy exit of a character. Dialogue reveals clues as well. We point out that something happened in the space between panels, and their ability to follow the story is a sign that they infer. A few lessons later, they are more comfortable with their own capacity to discern the "between the lines" and we begin to introduce text examples to supplant the visuals.

We also like Laura Robb's inference game (2000). A small group acts out an event, such as two students pointing and laughing at something outside, then stopping immediately when a third student joins them. The rest of the class has to use their inferential thinking to explain what they think is happening in the scene. We ask them to speculate on what the actors' motives might be and then we make the link to background knowledge explicit by challenging students to explain their reasoning. To solidify their understanding, we often ask students to compose a passage describing the event. This allows us to check for understanding and to determine which students might still need instruction.

What we've learned from our students is that inferencing takes time. It also requires a great deal of modeling. Our experience suggests that modeling inferences occurs best in small groups or with individual students. As we stated above, we also know that inferences are based on background knowledge and engagement with the text. As Winne, Graham, and Prock (1993) pointed out, inferences are based on either declarative or procedural knowledge. Inferences based on declarative knowledge are not as often a challenge. It's easy to understand that Kaila's declarative knowledge about the solar system helps her infer meaning from a text she's reading about the moon. Inferences that require significant levels of procedural knowledge and less background knowledge are often more difficult for students to make. For example, it's easy to understand Jerome's confusion about Hattie not wanting to sell her claim to Traft Martin. The author of *Hattie Big Sky* (Larson, 2006) doesn't specifically identify why Hattie doesn't want to sell her land to a nearby rancher. Through a discussion about the consequences of selling the land that we had with Jerome, he began to infer that Hattie had too much pride to sell her land, didn't want to leave her new friends, and was fearful about the uncertainty of having a place to live.

Source: Jacket cover from *Hattie Big Sky* by Kirby Larson. Used by permission of Random House Children's Books, a division of Random House, Inc.

As with so many strategies, students need to have them modeled and explained. They also need extensive practice trying on the strategy, with feedback from the teacher. Over time, the strategy will become a habit. Taken together with all of the other skills outlined in this chapter, students will become great readers who use what they know.

MOVING FROM GOOD TO GREAT

The habit of using what they know is a synthesis of the comprehension strategies we teach to students around activating background knowledge, making connections, building vocabulary and concept knowledge, and making inferences. However, if taught in isolation for too long, they become detached from authentic reading and reinforce for children that reading is work, and drudgery at that. Great readers skillfully weave all of these processes in ways that don't end up interfering with their purposes for reading. Therefore we model these strategies, first individually, and then in conjunction with other processes. We still need to cause readers to notice these processes, to lift them out of their reading from time to time in order to foster their metacognitive awareness. Conferring with students is one of the best ways to hold rich conversations that cause this noticing. The metacognitive questions you'll find in Figure 4.2 are the ones we keep close by to help us ask good questions to encourage them to use what they know. These questions aren't intended to scaffold use of the strategy, but to foster self-awareness. Although there are columns for each of the four habits discussed in this chapter, we hope you notice how some of the questions reach across habits, such as asking the child what the author could do on that last page that would be a surprise. Perhaps this habit is the one closest to our teacher hearts, because it speaks to us as well—use what you know in order to understand.

Does the student:

Make Connections
- Understand why his or her connection may be different from another reader's connection?
- Identify how a connection helps make sense of text?
- Make appropriate and relevant connections?

Activate Background Knowledge
- Evaluate the usefulness of specific background knowledge?
- Name different ways to activate background knowledge?
- Ask questions that would lead to building background knowledge?
- Implement various previewing techniques to determine which aspect of background knowledge is most important and helpful?
- Recognize new information while reading, and revise background knowledge to accommodate this new information?

Build Vocabulary and Concept Knowledge
- Use context clues to identify the meaning of a word?
- Use morphemic knowledge or identify the meaning of a word?
- Substitute words appropriately to check meaning?

FIGURE 4.2 Metacognitive Questions

Metacognition About Making Connections	Metacognition About Activating Background Knowledge	Metacognition About Building Vocabulary and Concept Knowledge	Metacognition About Making Inferences
Guiding Questions for Assessing the Student: Does the child demonstrate a broad range of connections, or just a single type (e.g., only personal connections)?	*Guiding Questions for Assessing the Student:* Can the child describe new information he or she learned from the text?	*Guiding Questions for Assessing the Student:* Can the child describe or demonstrate how he or she figures out an unfamiliar word or phrase?	*Guiding Questions for Assessing the Student:* Does the child add correct information not explicitly offered in the text?
Does the child notice his or her connections?	Does the child specify what he or she wants to learn from a text before beginning it?	Does the child connect vocabulary to concepts?	Can the child make predictions or draw conclusions in advance of the ending?
Questions to Ask the Student: Think about the last book you read in independent reading. Did it remind you of anything? What did it remind you of?	*Questions to Ask the Student:* How do the pictures on a book cover help you get your mind ready to read?	*Questions to Ask the Student:* How does recognizing a word in the title help you figure out what the book might be about?	*Questions to Ask the Student:* What is important for a poet to really think about the words he or she uses in a poem?
Why is it helpful to make connections to books as you read them?	Do pictures in a book help you figure out what you know about a topic?	What is happening in this picture? What does it tell you about the words you might find on this page?	How can making a picture in your mind help you understand what you read?
What connections did you make to this book?	How can the words in the text help you remember what you know about a topic?	Why is it important to use what you know to figure out a new word?	What should you do if something you read doesn't make sense?
What kinds of connections help you understand what you read?	Why is it good to talk to someone about what you are reading?	Why is helpful to notice when words in a book repeat?	How do words that describe a character help you get to know that character?
Why is it helpful for readers to make connections to other books?	How can reading help you learn new things?	What could the author do to surprise you on the last page of a book?	

Make Inferences

- Use text clues and prior knowledge to make an inference?
- Identify a previous inference that was made and revise it, if necessary?

Professional Development

1. Use the lens of background knowledge to reconsider the books that are assigned reading or read-alouds. Ask your local children's librarian or bookstore to recommend books written by local authors. If you have several students from another country, consider adding books set in their homeland.
2. Select one picture book to read aloud to several classes (perhaps across the grades). Before reading, brainstorm with students what background knowledge they have on the topic. At a faculty meeting, compare the lists. What similarities/differences do you see from class to class, grade to grade. How would these differences impact your teaching?
3. Introduce the "inference game" to families. We've seen it become a favorite activity at birthday parties and family get-togethers.

References

Baumann, J. F., Edwards, E. C., Font, G., Tereshinski, C. A., Kame'enui, E. J., & Olejnik, S. (2002). Teaching morphemic and contextual analysis to fifth-grade students. *Reading Research Quarterly, 37*, 150–176.

Beck, I. L., Perfetti, C. A., & McKeown, M. G. (1982). The effects of long-term vocabulary instruction on lexical access and reading comprehension. *Journal of Educational Psychology, 74*, 506–521.

Blachowicz, C. L. Z., & Fisher, P. (2000). Vocabulary instruction. In M. L. Kamil, P. B. Mosenthal, P. D. Pearson, & R. Barr (Eds.), *Handbook of reading research* (Vol. III, pp. 503–523). Mahwah, NJ: Lawrence A. Erlbaum.

Bonin, F., Devaux, B., & Dupré, A. (2006). *Turtles of the world.* Baltimore: Johns Hopkins University Press.

Brassell, D., & Flood, J. (2004). *Vocabulary strategies every teacher needs to know.* San Diego, CA: Academic Professional Development.

Collins, A., Brown, I., & Larkin, K. (1980). Inferences in text understanding. In R. J. Spiro, B. C. Bruce, & W. F. Brewer (Eds.), *Theoretical issues in teaching comprehension* (pp. 385–407). Hillsdale, NJ: Lawrence A. Erlbaum.

Farley, M. J., & Elmore, P. B. (1992). The relationship of reading comprehension to critical thinking skills, cognitive ability, and vocabulary for a sample of underachieving college freshman. *Educational and Psychological Measurement, 52*, 921–931.

Fisher, D., & Frey, N. (in press). Word wise and content rich. Portsmouth, NH: Heinemann.

Forbes, E. (1998). *Johnny Tremain.* Boston: Houghton Mifflin.

Frey, N., & Fisher, D. (2007). *Reading for information in elementary school: Content literacy strategies to build comprehension.* Upper Saddle River, NJ: Merrill Prentice Hall.

Hall, D. (1983). *Ox-cart man.* New York: Puffin.

Keene, E. O., & Zimmermann, S. (2007). *Mosaic of thought: The power of comprehension strategy instruction* (2nd ed.). Portsmouth, NH: Heinemann.

Kintsch, W. (2004). The construction-integration model of text comprehension and its implications for instruction. In R. R. Ruddell & N. J. Unrath (Eds.), *Theoretical models and processes of reading* (5th ed., pp. 1270–1328). Newark, DE: International Reading Association.

Larson, K. (2006). *Hattie big sky.* New York: Delacorte.

McKoon, G., & Ratcliff, R. (1992). Inference during reading. *Psychological Review, 99*(3), 440–466.

Morris, A. (1995). *Houses and homes.* New York: HarperTrophy.

Murray, S. (2005). *Eyewitness: American Revolution.* New York: DK Publishing.

Nelson, P. (2003). *Left for dead: One young man's search for justice for the USS Indianapolis.* New York: Delacorte.

Pressley, M. (2000). What should comprehension instruction be the instruction of? In M. L. Kamil, P. B. Mosenthal, P. D. Pearson, & R. Barr (Eds.), *Handbook of reading research* (Vol. III, pp. 545–562). Mahwah, NJ: Lawrence A. Erlbaum.

Robb, L. (2000). *Teaching reading in middle school.* New York: Scholastic.

Stahl, S. (1983). Differential knowledge and reading comprehension. *Journal of Reading Behavior, 15*, 33–50.

Taba, H. (1967). *Teacher's handbook for elementary social studies.* Boston: Allyn & Bacon.

Tolhurst, M. (1998). *The explorer's handbook: How to become an intrepid traveler.* New York: Dutton.

Weaver, C. A., & Kintsch, W. (1991). Expository text. In R. Barr, M. L. Kamil, P. B. Mosenthal, & P. D. Pearson (Eds.), *Handbook of reading research* (Vol. II, pp. 230–245). New York: Longman.

White, E. B. (1952). *Charlotte's web.* New York: Harper.

Wilhelm, J. (2001). *Improving comprehension with think-aloud strategies: Modeling what good readers do.* New York: Scholastic.

Winne, P. H., Graham, L., & Prock, L. (1993). A model of poor readers' text-based inferencing: Effects of explanatory feedback. *Reading Research Quarterly, 28*, 52–66.

CHAPTER 5

Great Readers Understand How Stories Work

Children learn about stories before coming to school. Adam fondly remembers his mother reading him fairy tales from an old, tattered edition of Grimm's fairy tales that had been passed down through the family. Every night, the same ritual: one tale before bed, and then lights out! *Little Red Cap* (aka *Little Red Riding Hood)* was his favorite. Nancy's daughter, Bridget, demanded to hear *The Poky Little Puppy* (Lowery, 1980) at least 400 times between her second and third birthdays. (According to *Publishers Weekly,* this is the best-selling children's book of all time, with more than 14,000,000 copies sold between 1942 and 2000.) Think about all that Adam and Bridget learned from hearing the same story read over and over again: Be careful of strangers (there might be a wolf in disguise); don't be late for dinner (you might miss the strawberry shortcake). Stories like these help children make sense of the world. For example, *Little Red Cap* helped Adam understand that there are good and bad people in the world. The need for story manifests itself from the beginning of a child's life, because a child needs to organize the world in order to understand it. Stories also serve as a scaffold for connecting previously learned lessons to new situations.

Anthropologists and historians have documented the archetypes present throughout the world in the folktales and legends of every culture. Creation stories are among the oldest, usually passed down through the oral tradition. Most contain a birth element to explain the beginning of the world, either through a higher power or because of a journey from either the sky or beneath the earth. *Pourquoi* stories were used to explain natural phenomenon, from why we have thunderstorms to why turtles have shells. Nearly every culture possesses trickster tales, notable Anansi the spider in Africa, the coyote in Native American tales, and birds of many kinds in Aesop's fables. The "Cinderella" fairy tales of a good young girl who is treated badly by others can be found in versions from around the world. For instance, the Mi'kmaq tribe of the Canadian Maritimes tells the story of "The Hidden One," a scarred and abused younger sister who is chosen as the wife of the Invisible Boy, a handsome youth with magical abilities. In this version of the story, a moccasin serves as the symbol of the perfect fit (Rand, 1894).

Many of these ancient stories were cautionary tales, warning of the dangers of being greedy, lazy, or vain. Anthropologists theorize that societies transmitted values from one generation to the next through such tales, thereby ensuring that order would reign for a few more years. Lest you think these cautionary tales are the product of a simpler time, you need only review your e-mail inbox. Chances are that it is jammed with the sort of stories that begin with, "This is really true, because it happened to the second cousin of one of my co-workers. . . ." These urban legends are the folktales of the modern world, and websites such as www.snopes.com stay busy investigating which are true and which are entertaining, but nonetheless fictional. (Hopefully, we can put to rest once and for all that the boy who played Mikey on the Life cereal commercials did *not* die due to an unfortunate mixture of Coca-Cola and PopRocks!)

UNDERSTANDING HOW STORIES WORK

Children come to us with an internalized sense of story, albeit one that is not part of their conscious thought. We know some might argue that not all of our students come from households where bedtime stories are a ritual, but even these students learn stories through family tales, television shows, and movies. Although we want to teach them the content of stories, we can't let this be our solitary goal. We also need to teach them to notice the elements that make a good story come to life. This means that children need to experience story in a variety of ways. First, they need to hear good tales read to them by an expert reader (you), and then they need to have opportunities to talk about the stories with you and their peers. Second, they need to tell and retell stories, as this allows them to further soak up the elements that make a story "just so." And we aren't talking about just the primary grades here—this goes from kindergarten all the way through middle school.

Nancy will always treasure the day that Ryan, a student with autism, launched into a retelling of *The Wonderful Wizard of Oz* (Baum, 2000) that can only be described as performance art. Ryan's ear for detail and his lively imagination came together in a magnificent way as he retold the tale using voices, gestures, and even other members of the class to make his story come to life. (Nancy was happy to be cast as Glinda, the good witch.) Of course, our students also need time to write about stories and create their own original tales. We've been entertained by Alex's original *pourquoi* on how the lion got its mane (suffice to say that it included a makeover show appearance). Even emergent readers are ready at a moment's notice to create an alternative ending to a familiar story. Doug will never read *The Paper Bag Princess* (Munsch, 1992) in quite the same way after listening to kindergartner Aamir's version in which the dragon quickly dispatched both the prince and the princess at the beginning of the story, then got on with the more interesting business of breathing fire, flying around, and defeating far more worthy opponents.

The habit of understanding how stories work involves recognizing the way authors construct stories to entertain, inform, caution, and provoke thought. Great readers are able to move beyond the content of the story itself to analyze the genre and appreciate the unique qualities offered in a text. In this chapter, we'll discuss the following aspects that build this habit.

John Graham

1. Understanding Story Elements
2. Identifying and Understanding Literary Devices
3. Understanding and Analyzing Characters
4. Understanding and Analyzing Setting and Plot
5. Understanding and Analyzing Theme

Understanding Story Elements

Elizabeth Sulzby was among the first to tell us about the knowledge young children possess about story even before they enter formal schooling. Ryan's retelling of *The Wonderful Wizard of Oz* echoes Sulzby's identification of *reenactment* and *dialogic storytelling* as a necessary element of understanding (Sulzby, 1985, p. 467). She noted that opportunities to perform the story (reenactment) and repeat important parts of the dialogue (dialogic) reinforced the child's recall and understanding of the piece, when compared to passive listening experiences. Knowledge of how stories work is important in reading comprehension as well, because students utilize story elements such as character, plot, setting, and theme to organize and sequence (Dimino, Taylor, & Gersten, 1995). We foster the habit of understanding how stories work by introducing, and then deepening, our student's understanding of these story elements.

Narrative stories have characteristics and structures that great readers utilize to understand what is written. These characteristics, referred to as story grammar, include characters, setting, problem, conflict, solution, and plot. Readers need to

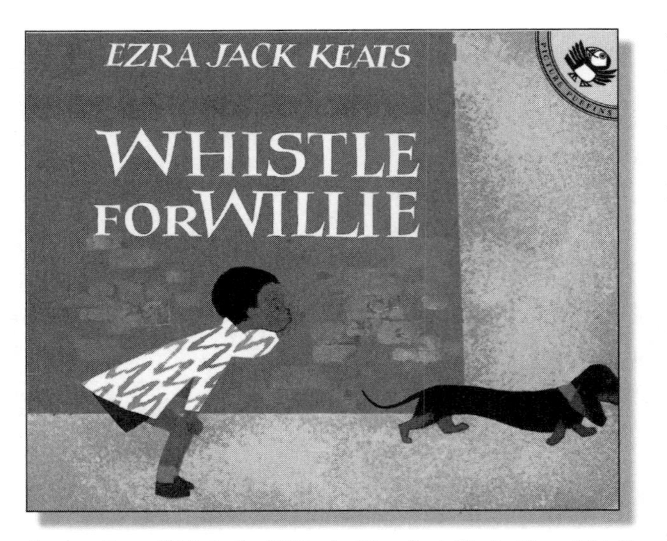

Source: From *Whistle for Willie*, by Ezra Jack Keats. Copyright © 1964 Penguin Group. Reprinted with permission.

understand these elements in order to anticipate story events, retell, and analyze. We know from our experience and from research that children who are instructed in these elements achieve higher levels of comprehension (Baumann & Bergeron, 1993; Davis, 1994).

This understanding of story elements emerges from repeated exposure and conversation about their use. While conducting a shared reading of *Whistle for Willie* (Keats, 1977), we tell students that we've noticed that Peter has a problem (he wishes he could whistle for his dog, Willie), and that we know that most stories contain a problem the main character must face. We also let our students in on the secret of literature—most stories contain a solution to the problem that is discoverable during reading. Nancy's first-grade students practice whistling to see if they have the same problem as Peter, and help one another to learn the fine art of whistling. Admittedly, it's a noisy lesson, but her students internalize the problem–solution construct of the story. And, more importantly, they develop an understanding of how this element works in other stories.

Children also need to apply their growing knowledge of story grammar to organize their thinking and support retellings. Young children can create story maps by illustrating each element. We rely on collaborative learning in literacy centers and stations as a vehicle to help students consolidate their thinking about new skills and strategies. Our Mapmaking Center is a popular one, a place where students work together to create graphic organizers of the narrative and informational texts they are reading. We stock it with the usual accoutrements—colorful paper, scissors, markers, and the like—and encourage students to illustrate and write about the elements used by the writer to frame the story they have just read. A general rule of thumb is that the smaller the child, the larger the paper. While older students can create these story maps in a conventional manner, using a pencil and an 8 ½ by 11 inch sheet of paper, the younger ones need big sheets of chart paper. The large size also encourages collaboration as each child takes a section of the map.

A story map that isn't utilized for anything beyond completion of the task is nothing more than a worksheet. You might as well just hand out dittos. The true purpose of the map, or any graphic organizer, is to serve as an intermediate tool for storing information. Once completed, we confer with children to listen to their retellings. We encourage them to use the story map they have created to plan their retelling and refer them back to their map when they have omitted a vital element.

Another goal of our story elements instruction is to ensure that students find the patterns across texts. A matrix of story elements is an easy way to visually organize this information for young readers. We list each element across the columns of the chart paper, with the titles of the books we are reading listed down the side as rows. As we finish books during shared reading, we list the names of the characters, the setting, the problem and solution, and so on. Over time, students see that all the stories have a setting, a plot, main characters, and a resolution to a problem. We talk about the ways they differ from one another across texts, so that each unique combination of elements results in a unique story. The commonalities are important as well. No story would hang together well without a beginning, middle, and end, or without the establishment of a character in a setting. By appreciating the ways in which writers utilize the common vocabulary of story elements in unique patterns, young writers can begin to apply these elements to their own creations.

Identifying and Understanding Literary Devices

Because the relationship between reading and writing is so important, readers also need to understand the literary devices authors use to make stories come alive. These devices are particularly useful for fostering mental imagery, an important strategy used by effective readers to support comprehension (Borduin, Borduin, & Manley, 1994). A list of common literary devices can be found in Figure 5.1.

In her book *When Writers Read*, Jane Hansen (2001) writes about her work with young writers as she and a group of teachers altered the ways in which they taught reading.

> When these children started to read high-quality literature, they not only appreciated it but also mined that print for ideas for their own writing. They found topics they could write about and borrowed authors' ways with words. (p. 3)

That mental image of mining evoked by Hansen is a powerful one, and a reminder to us as teachers about the connection that is possible between reading and writing, if only we would allow it to occur. When we talk about teaching literary devices, we are not speaking of the lifeless lessons of English classrooms of the past, where the writer's words were wrung of any life by the dispassionate analysis of foreshadowing and flashback. It's not only about memorizing the difference between simile and metaphor—teach it so they answer it correctly on the standardized test, then move on. It's about admiring the wonder of a metaphor when Beatrice Schenk de Regniers reminds us to "Keep a Poem in Your Pocket" because "the little poem will sing to you" (Hajdusiewicz, 1990, p. 163).

We use poems a great deal when teaching about literary devices because the nature of the genre requires the use of powerful language. This concentrated language pops off the page and out of the mouths of readers, who play with the delicious imagery through voice and movement. The poem "Cat" by Mary Britton Miller (Hajdusiewicz, 1990, p. 33) is a good example.

The cat "yawns" and "stretches" and "stands on four stiff legs." First-graders love to mimic the movements of an awakening cat, and we talk about the similarity to us as we get out of bed in the morning. We use our voices to elongate the words *yawn* and *stretch* because we think the poet wanted us to slow down as we spoke those words. We then write another version of the poem, this time starring a dog. How does he move differently? Lexi told us her dog walks in a circle three times before he lays down, so we include this in our poem. Kevin makes motions like an airplane circling in the sky, and we add that as well.

FIGURE 5.1 Literary Elements

Literary Device	Definition and Example
Allegory	A story that is used to teach something. Usually the stories are long and require analysis to find the allegory or intention. *Example:* Parables in the Bible and Aesop's fables.
Alliteration	Same letter or sound to start each word in a string. Used frequently in books for emergent readers in part to foster phonemic awareness. *Example:* "Andrea anxiously awaited arrangement."
Allusion	A reference to a well-known person, myth, historical event, or biblical story. *Example:* "She's just like Narcissus" or "It's as bad as the sinking of the *Titanic*."
Flashback	Pauses the action to comment or portray a scene that took place earlier. *Example:* During a scene in which a person walks through a dark alley, the author pauses to relate a story about another time the character was scared.
Foreshadowing	A hint of things to come—usually, but not always, an unpleasant event. *Example:* Early in a story, a character receives a letter from a long-lost relative, who later appears in the story.
Hyperbole	An exaggerated comment or line used for effect and not meant to be taken literally. *Example:* When faced with a long line at the Department of Motor Vehicles, Andrew said, "It will take an eternity to be allowed to drive."
Imagery	Involves language that evokes one or all of the five senses: seeing, hearing, tasting, smelling, touching. *Examples:* "Her lips taste of honey and dew" or "Walking through the halls, amid the crashing sound of lockers closing and the smell of yesterday's coffee, I saw the radiant teacher."
Irony and satire	Use of sophisticated humor in relaying a message, often saying what something is when the opposite or reverse could be true. Authors use irony to say one thing when they mean another. *Example:* James is looking at the shark bite out of his surfboard and says, "Finally, I've got a short board." Satire focuses more on mockery or wit to attack or ridicule something. *Example:* "Very graceful," Ted remarked, when Craig slipped and fell on an icy patch.
Metaphor	In contrast with similes, metaphors make a direct statement and do not use "like" or "as" to make the comparison. Metaphors simply make a comparison in which one thing is said to be another. *Example:* "The dog's fur was electric, standing on end in fear."
Personification	When authors give animals, ideas, or actions the qualities of humans, we call it personification. This is common in Disney films as well as with children's authors. *Example:* Molly the rabbit said, "These carrots are the best ever!" Personification is also used for more abstract ideas. *Example:* "Hate has you trapped in her arms."

Point of view	In first person, the story is told from the perspective of the narrator and we readers cannot know or witness anything the narrator does not tell us. *Example:* "I walked quietly into the dark room, fearful of awakening the sleeping children." In second person, the narrator speaks directly to the reader. *Example:* "You will likely know by now that Andre is a bad guy." In third person, the narrator is omniscient (all-knowing) and can convey different perspectives at different times. *Example:* "Petra was angered by Jennifer's words, while Jennifer had no idea that her friend was seething."
Simile	A statement in which two things are compared and said to be *like* or *as* another. *Example:* "Like a rain-filled cloud, Anna cried and cried when she learned of her lost fortune."
Symbolism	An object or action that means something more than its literal meaning. *Example:* When an author introduces a black crow into the text, readers are prepared for death. This compares with the sighting of a white dove, which conveys peace or life to readers.
Tone and mood	Attitude an author takes toward a subject or character such as hateful, serious, humorous, sarcastic, solemn, objective, conveys the tone or mood. The author can use dialogue, settings, or descriptions to set a tone or mood.

Source: Adapted from Frey, N., & Fisher, D. (2006). *Language arts workshop: Purposeful reading and writing instruction.* Upper Saddle River, NJ: Merrill Prentice Hall.

Dog

The dog
Sniffs around to find
A comfortable spot
Looks to see
If anyone watches
Turns three times
Circling like an airplane
Lands on a soft spot
And closes his eyes goodnight.

We look for the rich language of literary devices in books as well. We discuss personification in *The Grouchy Ladybug* (Carle, 1996), enjoy the onomatopoeia utilized in comic books (*Bam! Pow! Zing!*), and admire the flashback technique used by Lois Lowery (1998) in *Number the Stars*. As we write, we consciously deploy these same techniques to tell original tales. Kindergarten student Sadie writes a story about a happy butterfly that finds something to celebrate each hour of the day, and draws a clock face in the corner of the pages just as Eric Carle taught her to do. Fifth-grader Arturo illustrates a series of panels about his favorite wrestler, inserting onomatopoeia such as "Wham!" to signal a punch and "Crack!" to denote the sound of a bone breaking. Fourth-grade student Roberta combines her social studies content of the Gold Rush to construct a short story of an original Forty-Niner telling his grandson about the first mining days at Sutter's Mill. As readers and writers, students acquire the habit of understanding how stories work by employing the devices used by writers. Our evidence of their understanding of literary devices is found in the footprints of the authors they have read and discussed. You see, good readers attempt to memorize literary devices, while great readers use these devices to share their thinking with the world.

Understanding and Analyzing Characters

Story elements comprise the scaffolding of a constructed story; our students must also understand the individual components in depth. Character development is essential to a well-told tale, and analyzing the motives, through dialogue and action, can lead students to a deeper understanding of how a character grows and changes across the story arc. As teachers, most of us have favorite characters that linger in our imagination long after the book has closed. Nancy has professed her admiration of Madeline, especially her fearlessness in the face of adversity (Bemelmans, 1954). Max, making mischief in his wolf suit, resonates with grown-up Doug, who has been known to be a bit mischievous himself (Sendak, 1992). Adam is one of the millions who are fascinated with shy, yet courageous Harry Potter (Rowling, 2007). But why do these characters speak to us across time? The answer lies in the way the character has been constructed, and how he or she speaks to a recognizable truth about the human condition. Of course, we're not talking to five-year-olds about resonance. We're asking them about the times when they have felt brave, or mischievous, or courageous.

The protagonist of the story often represents the author's voice, so we talk about purpose as it relates to character. Author's purpose is a tricky proposition for young readers, who are more oriented toward the story itself than its deconstruction. However, it is appropriate to discuss why the author chose his or her main character. Asking questions like, "Do you think the character is like, or unlike, the author?" can elicit surprisingly thoughtful comments. Nancy posed this question to Regina after she read *Dear Mr. Blueberry* (James, 1996). The story is told through a series of letters over summer vacation between Emily and her teacher, concerning the whale she has discovered in her backyard pond. Like most skeptical adults, Mr. Blueberry first humors Emily, then explains in an increasingly strident tone why there can't possibly be a whale in the pond. Ever cheerful, Emily disregards the cynicism and blithely continues to ask questions about the care and feeding of this unexpected visitor. As readers, we can see that Emily is correct, and we enjoy Mr. Blueberry's consternation. When asked which character the author resembled, Regina answered immediately. "Mr. Blueberry," she said. "He's probably been wrong when a kid was right the whole time." Indeed.

Authors use the words and actions of a character to illustrate his or her motives, interests, and conflicts. Therefore, we return to analysis of dialogue and actions as we read to and with our students. When Max shouts at his mother, "I'll eat you up!" he is

Source: Reprinted with the permission of Margret K. McElderry Books, an imprint of Simon & Schuster Children's publishing Division from DEAR MR. BLUEBERRY by Simon James. Copyright © 1991 Simon James.

showing his anger at her directive to come to supper. Madeline's enjoyment of the adventure of having an appendectomy speaks volumes about her disposition. Harry's ability to stand up to Lord Voldermort time and time again shows us his courage.

Talking with readers about how we figure out the nature of a character through words and actions enlivens their writing as well. We point out that authors rarely tell us, "Madeline is the bravest little girl ever" or "Max figures out how to handle his own anger by dealing with the wild things." Instead, we challenge our students to identify how authors animate their characters, giving them dialogue to speak and actions to perform. In their original writing, we encourage students to show us how the magician is clever, or the old woman is wise, or the sailor is secretly afraid of water.

Older readers are ready for more complex analysis of characters in story, and fortunately there is an abundance of quality children's literature that doesn't insult its young readers with cardboard characters spouting improbable platitudes. Leah, a fourth-grader we know, read Kate Di Camillo's (2000) *Because of Winn-Dixie* and immediately wanted to read other books by this author. She next read *The Tale of Despereaux* (Di Camillo, 2003) and told us she liked it less, in part because of the character development. "I don't know, Despereaux's just a little *too* good, you know? Like, I had a hard time believing in him. He doesn't seem to get angry, even when he should." Importantly, Leah wasn't about to give up on this author, because she knew how magical DiCamillo's writing can be. When *The Miraculous Journey of Edward Tulane* (2006) arrived in our mailbox, we knew we had found the book for Leah. This was a character she could sink her teeth into—flawed, self-absorbed—who undergoes a transformation of character. Leah didn't disappoint us either. When we met to talk with her about the book, she told us:

> I *so* didn't like Edward at the beginning of the book, and I wasn't even sure I wanted to read it. Who wants to read about someone you don't like? But then I was thinking about what Kate DiCamillo might make Edward do. I think she wanted us to see that people can change, and they can get better through their life. It was like he had to lose everything he thought was important before he could see what really was important.

Leah's response is a reminder about the habits of great readers, and how they are consolidated over time. Clearly Leah has a strong sense of character development. But she also utilized her understanding of the author's works. She monitored her own responses to the reading, noting when they shifted and connecting it back to the author's purpose. She also saw herself as a reader, one with the stamina to persist when the book got a bit rocky for her. These are the moments when you get to witness a reader moving from good to great.

FIGURE 5.2 Questions for Analyzing a Character

Making Personal Connections with Characters	• Do you like or dislike this character? Why? • Does he or she remind you of yourself? • Does he or she remind you of someone you know?
Richness of Character Development	• Does this character act and speak in a believable way? • How has he or she changed during the story? • Do the reactions of other characters toward him or her change over time? In what ways? • Does your character get what he or she deserves, or not?
Character Motivation	• Why do you think this character is the way he or she is? Did something happen to him or her? • What does this character want or need? Why? • Is his or her goal realistic? • Do you expect him or her to reach this goal? Why?
The Writer's Craft	• How do you describe the character? • In what ways do you tell about the character using dialogue? • What actions does the character take that lets you know the kind of person he or she is? • What do other characters say and think that lets you know about the kind of person he or she is? • Why did you create this character?

Some of you are probably in awe of Leah, and incredulous that many, or perhaps any, of your students will analyze stories at such a deep level. Trust us, and trust your students. If you provide multiple exposures to stories, lots of opportunities for scaffolded conversations about books, and you teach students the language of story grammar, it will happen.

We want students to incorporate their growing understanding of character development in their own writing. We also recognize that this understanding springs from the conversations we have with them (see Figure 5.2). These questions remind us about how writers interact with the characters they create. Do you like the character you've created, or not? Does the character deserve what happens to him in your story, or is it a cruel fate? When our students see themselves as writers making choices about how their characters behave, they recognize that the authors they read have done likewise.

Understanding and Analyzing Setting and Plot

Setting and plot are part of the story grammar, but often function at a less conspicuous level for young readers. The setting of the story describes both when and where the story takes place. However, the setting of a good story is more than just a dot on a map and a tick on a timeline. Just telling our students this simple definition won't help them to understand how integral setting is to the characters and the plot, even though providing a simple definition is the first step. No less a writer than Eudora Welty (1998) said, "[E]very story would be another story, and unrecognizable as art if it took up its characters and plot and happened somewhere else" (p. 787). Can you imagine *The Hunchback of Notre Dame* (Hugo, 2002) without the backdrop of Paris? On the first pages of the novel, Hugo contrasts the grandeur of the city with its overpopulation. He describes the palace yard as "crowded with people [who] looked like a sea, into which five or six streets, like the mouths of so many rivers, disgorged their living streams. The waves of this sea, incessantly swelled by new arrivals, broke against the corners of the houses, projecting here and there like promontories into the irregular basin of the square" (p. 6). Is it any wonder then that Quasimodo would seek the sanctuary of the bell tower, high above the crowds and away from their stares? Paris in the 15th century is used by Hugo to describe all that is wrong with a society that judges Quasimodo so carelessly. Transport Quasimodo to New York City, and he might be mistaken for just another punk rocker.

Setting is no less important in children's stories than in the classics of adult fiction. The labor versus management conflict of *Click, Clack, Moo: Cows That Type* (Cronin, 2002) can only take place on a farm—any other setting would leave the reader bewildered. A brigantine called the *Seahawk* and the oppressive expectations of English girls in 1832 play integral parts in *The True Confessions of Charlotte Doyle* (Avi, 2005), and a reader's inattention to either would result in a loss of meaning. Changes in the setting can signal an important turn of events, as when a hailstorm destroys the crops in *Hattie Big Sky* (Larson, 2006), thus mirroring the storm of conflicts between characters in the story.

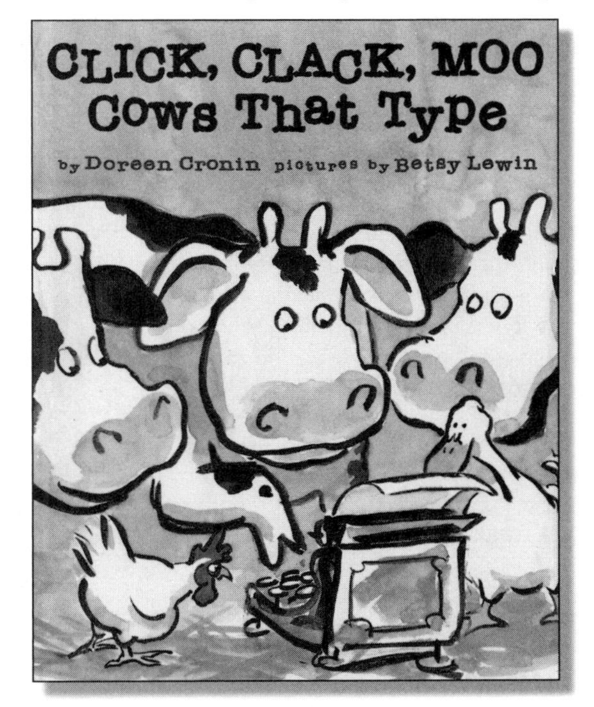

Source: Reprinted with permission of Simon & Schuster for Young Readers, an imprint of Simon & Schuster Children's Publishing Division from *Click, Clack, Moo: Cows That Type* by Doreen Cronin, illustrated by Betsy Lewin. Jacket illustrations copyright © 2000 Betsy Lewin.

As we read with students, we stop to think aloud about the way the author uses setting as a way to represent the ideas in the story. For example, when Doug speaks of *Hatchet* (Paulsen, 2006), he remarks on the isolation of the physical setting and how that mirrors the loneliness Brian was experiencing even before the plane crashed in the remote Alaska wilderness. When Brian is able to create a shelter for himself, Doug thinks aloud with students about Brian's need for a home in the wake of his parents' divorce. Doug invites students to think aloud as well, commenting on the elements of the story as they arise. Romel's observation that "the wilderness is like his [Brian's] life, 'cause he doesn't know how to escape his life now that his parents split up" lets Doug know that Romel is analyzing the setting at a sophisticated level and like a great reader.

Like setting, plot interacts with the overall story and (hopefully) propels the reader forward through the book. The plot of a story is more than the sequence of events, although this is where we begin with young readers. A good plot contains an element of suspense, even if it is not a suspense novel. It includes unexpected events, usually characterized as "twists" that surprise and intrigue without leaving the reader incredulous. It may contain cliffhangers that cause the reader to move quickly to the next chapter.

Conversations with our youngest readers revolve around the sequence of the plot, especially beginning, middle, and end. Fairy tales and folktales work well for these purposes, especially because many of them contain useful signal words like *first*, *next*, *last*, *before*, *after*, *next*, and *finally*. Stories containing numbers, such as *The Three Little Pigs*, and sequence stories like *Joseph Had a Little Overcoat* (Taback, 1999) reinforce the importance of stringing together a progression of events to recall and retell. We ask students to create a simple illustration of each event in the plot and then collect them all to use as a whole group to retell the story. We like to use their work, rather than preprinted sequence cards, because this drawing-to-learn activity seems to strengthen their visual memory.

Older readers learn about plot devices like cliffhangers, hooks, and unexpected events. We've had great success with the *Choose Your Own Adventure* series in illustrating the decisions writers must make in advancing the plot. For example, *The Abominable Snowman* (Montgomery, 2006) offers a total of 27 different plot choices in this slim book. Who can resist this choice? "If you decide to go ahead with the expedition for the Yeti, turn to page 16. If you decide to postpone the expedition to let the Yeti calm down and go on to the Terai region in search of tigers, turn to page 19" (p. 10). Several of our students even write their own versions of *Choose Your Own Adventure*, such as Brittany, who set her tale at the Nickelodeon Kids Choice Award show and wrote plot choices that would variously lead you to a press conference with Justin Timberlake, presenting an award with Amanda Bynes, or getting slimed (a tradition on this network).

Eventually, we introduce more formal language around plot, especially as it applies to literary analysis. Students learn about exposition, rising action, climax, falling action, and denouement. The dramatic structure of story is known as Freytag's analysis, and this five-act sequence is found commonly throughout literature. The story maps of the first years of school give way to a new kind of mapping, such as that found in Figure 5.3. It's always wise to begin with what they know, so we introduce these terms using picture books and film. We read familiar fairy tales and map the dramatic arc of *Rapunzel* and *Rumpelstiltskin*. We discuss the way the

FIGURE 5.3 Narrative Structure

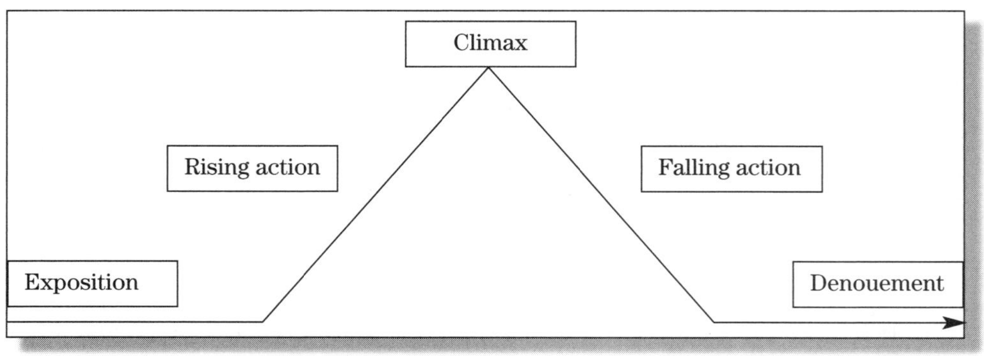

plot unfolds in familiar stories like *Charlotte's Web* (White, 2004) and view half-hour television episodes of *I Love Lucy* (the "Job Switching" episode from Season 2 featuring the automated chocolate factory scene works particularly well). Over time, the habit of recognizing the dramatic structure of a longer piece of text emerges. We have noted that while middle school students have been exposed to thousands of hours of narrative experiences, the introduction of the formal language of Freytag's analysis causes many of them to freeze in their tracks. By lowering the affective filter through a return to more familiar (and shorter) narrative, students easily assimilate the new vocabulary to the patterns they have grown to recognize.

Understanding and Analyzing Theme

Theme is perhaps the most difficult story element to teach and learn, in part because it cannot be viewed until after the reading is complete. It is the message of the piece, often told as a lesson or cautionary tale. In other cases, it is a comment on a universal truth, such as the ability of a hero to arise to a challenge. This element often gets tangled up in the minds of young readers with the plot or the subject of the story. Comparing and contrasting these two elements helps children see the difference between the two. Simple picture books offer an excellent opportunity for such comparisons. For example, most readers understand that *The Paper Bag Princess* (Munsch, 1992) is about a princess who is mistaken for a pauper by a snobby prince because of her disheveled appearance. That's the plot. But the theme is a reminder to not judge a book by its cover—a theme immortalized in thousands of stories from *The Frog Prince*, *Cinderella*, *The Tale of Despereaux* (DiCamillo, 2003), to *The Hunchback of Notre Dame* (Hugo, 2002).

But how do readers recognize these themes that arch over whole stories? We begin our conversations about theme by looking at the shortest of stories—the folktales and fables we discussed at the beginning of this chapter. These morality tales, some thousands of years old, resonate with young children as they spark a note of recognition about human foibles. Many contain outright statements of theme in the form of the moral to a story—"idleness brings want" in *The Ant and the Grasshopper*, "no act of kindness is ever wasted" in *The Lion and the Mouse*. We collect and catalog themes as we read these tales throughout the year. Sentence strips are labeled, and students attach titles they have read that contain similar themes. For example, Nancy's class of sixth-graders a few years ago assembled the following themes.

- A true friend is a friend forever.
- Nature is fragile but also dangerous.
- Knowledge is power.
- You can't judge a book by its cover.
- Inside each adult is an inner child.
- Adversity brings out the best in some people.
- War is cruel, especially to innocents.
- Growing up can be painful, but it is worth it.

- The loyalty of a pet is a strong one.
- Those who do not risk often regret.
- Love conquers all.
- You must be true to yourself, even if it means defying others.
- With many privileges come many responsibilities.
- Education can open a new world to a person.
- Growing up means leaving childhood behind.
- Good and evil exist in every person.
- Power can corrupt.
- Hate damages the person who hates, more than the person who is hated.

The Greek myths offer the same potential for older readers as the fables do for younger students. The legends of Hercules, for example, offer students a glimpse of the dangers of power without a sense of responsibility. Narcissus illustrates the peril of indulgent self-love. Exposure to the mythology in middle school also grounds students firmly in the background knowledge they will need to read deeply in high school and beyond. Literary works across the centuries, from Shakespeare, to Ralph Ellison, to Joyce Carol Oates, echo with the themes first recorded in Greek mythology. Creating a list of universal themes and cataloging books read by students in the class to these themes reinforces their understanding of the use of this element in longer texts. The great reader knows this and is always in search of universal themes.

MOVING FROM GOOD TO GREAT

Great readers know that stories help them understand themselves and the world around them. Great readers understand that literature serves as both a window and a mirror. Great readers use literature as a mirror to see themselves and to learn about their culture and traditions. They also use literature as a window to peer into the lives of others because literature allows them to meet people they'll never meet and visit places they never go. Adam can't help but think about Harry Potter, who he would have never met had J. K. Rowling not made the introduction. And today, Harry Potter is very much a part of Adam's life.

Great readers also have ways for thinking about the stories they read and for identifying the universal themes that authors write about. Great readers don't stop to focus on literary devices, for example, but instead use these devices to facilitate their understanding.

Does the student:

Understand Story Elements

- Explain why identifying the initiating event can help a reader understand the story?
- Describe the beginning, middle, and end of a story?

- Identify the basic elements of the story (characters, plot, setting, problem, and solution)?
- Use these elements to retell?
- Use the contents page to keep track of story events?
- Use a chapter title to make predictions and keep track of story events?

Identify and Understand Literary Devices
- Identify words or ideas that signal personification?
- Recognize alliteration?
- Recognize a pun?
- Recognize onomatopoeia?
- Recognize when authors contrast images?
- Recognize understatement?
- Use similes and metaphors in their oral and written language?
- Relate the use of flashback and foreshadowing to the author's craft?

Understand and Analyze Characters
- Discuss the relationships between characters?
- Identify who is speaking in a dialogue?
- Identify ways to infer the relationship between and among characters?
- Use a character's words and actions to make inferences about the character?
- Use dialogue to infer characters' feelings toward one another?
- Identify a character's plan for solving a problem?
- Relate character to plot?
- Explain how the problem and solution affect the character's actions?

Understand and Analyze Plot and Setting
- Identify the plot?
- Recognize how characters influence the plot?
- Apply Freytag's narrative structure to a story?
- Identify the setting?
- State why the setting is essential to the story?
- Relate plot, setting, and theme to one another?

Understand and Analyze Theme
- Identify the theme of the story?
- Discriminate between plot and theme?
- Name other stories with similar themes?
- Recognize the universality of major themes?
- Relate the author's purpose to the theme?

Professional Development

1. Buddy up younger grades with older, and have the older students write stories for their buddies. Instruct the older students that part of their task is help their buddies learn about story grammar.
2. Devote a faculty meeting to mapping out a developmental sequence for teaching story elements. Don't shy away from teaching terms to students, just make sure to provide developmentally appropriate examples. Create a glossary of terms, so that teachers use common terminology across the grades.
3. Invite community members to create posters that feature favorite literacy characters. Display the posters throughout the school.
4. Invite middle school and high school English teachers to a faculty meeting to discuss how they teach story grammar. It's helpful for all teachers to see how our expectations/benchmarks change and develop over time.

References

Avi. (2005). *The true confessions of Charlotte Doyle.* New York: HarperTrophy.

Baum, F. L. (2000). *The wonderful wizard of Oz.* New York: HarperCollins.

Baumann, J. F., & Bergeron, B. S. (1993). Story map instruction using children's literature: Effects on first graders' comprehension of central narrative elements. *Journal of Reading Behavior, 25*, 407–437.

Bemelmans, L. (1954). *Madeline.* New York: Simon and Schuster.

Borduin, B. J., Borduin, C. M. (1994). The use of imagery training to improve reading comprehension of second graders. *Journal of Genetic Psychology, 155*(1), 115–118.

Carle, E. (1996). *The grouchy ladybug.* New York: HarperTrophy.

Cronin, D. (2002). *Click, clack, moo: Cows that type.* New York: Simon & Schuster.

Davis, Z. T. (1994). Effects of prereading story-mapping on elementary readers' comprehension. *Journal of Educational Research, 87*, 353–360.

DiCamillo, K. (2000). *Because of Winn-Dixie.* Cambridge, MA: Candlewick.

DiCamillo, K. (2003). *The tale of Despereaux.* Cambridge, MA: Candlewick.

DiCamillo, K. (2006). *The miraculous journey of Edward Tulane.* Cambridge, MA: Candlewick.

Dimino, J. A., Taylor, R. M., & Gersten, R. M. (1995). Synthesis of research on story-grammar as a means to increase comprehension. *Reading & Writing Quarterly: Overcoming Learning Difficulties, 11*, 53–72.

Hajdusiewicz, B. B. (1990). *Poetry works! Idea book.* Parsippany, NJ: Modern Curriculum Press.

Hansen, J. (2001). *When writers read* (2nd ed.). Portsmouth, NH: Heinemann.

Hugo, V. (2002). *The hunchback of Notre Dame.* New York: Modern Library.

James, S. (1996). *Dear Mr. Blueberry.* New York: Aladdin.

Keats, E. J. (1977). *Whistle for Willie.* New York: Puffin.

Larson, K. (2006). *Hattie big sky.* New York: Delacorte.

Lowery, J. S. (1980). *The poky little puppy.* New York: Golden Books.

Lowry, L. (1998). *Number the stars.* New York: Laurel Leaf.

Montgomery, R. A. (2006). *The abominable snowman: Choose your own adventure #1.* Warren, VT: Chooseco.

Munsch, R. (1992). *The paper bag princess.* Toronto, Canada: Annick Press.

Paulsen, G. (2006). *Hatchet.* New York: Aladdin.

Rand, S. T. (1894). *Legends of the Micmac* (Vol. 1). New York: Longmans, Green, & Co.

Rowling, J. K. (2007). *Harry Potter and the deathly hallows.* New York: Scholastic.

Sendak, M. (1992). *Where the wild things are.* New York: HarperFestival.

Sulzby, E. (1985). Children's emergent reading of favorite storybooks: A developmental study. *Reading Research Quarterly, 20*, 458–481.

Taback, S. (1999). *Joseph had a little overcoat.* New York: Viking.

Welty, E. (1998). Place in fiction. In R. Ford & M. Kreyling (Eds.), *Eudora Welty: Stories, essays, and memoir* (pp. 781–796). New York: Library of America.

White, E. B. (2004). *Charlotte's web.* New York: HarperTrophy.

CHAPTER 6

Great Readers Read to Learn

Here's a quick quiz. Think about the last piece of nonfiction text you read (besides this book). It could be a magazine, book, newspaper, pamphlet, website, or a set of directions. Okay, got it? Fill out the information below.

- What was your purpose for reading this text?
- Did you read the whole text, or just parts of it?
- Before you read the text, did you make predictions or think about what type of information the piece might include?
- Did the text have any text features, such as graphs, charts, or tables?

Before he started to write this chapter, Adam was at the airport waiting for a flight. While browsing at the newsstand, he noticed a *Time Magazine* cover featuring an image of a chalkboard with the words, "Report Card on No Child Left Behind." In smaller letters, he read, "The sweeping federal law has brought more accountability to American schools, but is it improving education? How it can go from a C to an A." Adam started to answer this question in his head. He thought about the many classrooms he had visited that had been affected by this legislation. You can probably infer why this article appealed to Adam. He's an educator. At the time we wrote this book, Congress was considering reauthorizing this bill. Adam was also interested in this article because he knew one of the coauthors, Claudia Wallis. Several times over the years Adam and Claudia had talked about the No Child Left Behind Act. Adam knew that Claudia had strong feelings about this legislation. He wondered how her opinions had influenced how she wrote the article.

Adam used the table of contents to find the article. He didn't want to read the whole magazine at that time, just the article about NCLB. Since the title of the article was on the cover, Adam knew that this would be a major story and knew that cover stories in *Time* can be long! So, before reading, Adam skimmed through the article to see what he was in for. As he glanced through the pages, he noticed photographs of mostly African American students in classrooms. He thought, "Hmm, looks like inner-city schools. I bet this article will discuss how this legislation addresses urban schools." He saw a line graph labeled "Slow Growth Overall," a bar graph labeled "Less Science and History," a chart labeled "Lower State Standards," and a chart labeled "Grading the Program." He also noticed the headings:

- How should we measure learning?
- Can we trust the states to set standards?
- Too much reading and math?

Based on these graphics and the headings, Adam predicted the article wouldn't paint a positive picture of the legislation.

Let's pause here. Why are we spending so much time describing Adam's reading experience? And why did we ask you to consider your own experience with nonfiction? As we've said in previous chapters, we want you to use your observations of great readers such as yourself as a starting point when determining what strategies to teach our students. We want instruction to be based on authentic strategies those readers use. We also want instruction to draw on experiences with authentic text.

Before you read our analysis of Adam's description, take some time to think about what you noticed. What did you learn from reading about Adam's experience that might guide your classroom instruction? Here are some of our observations:

Hope Madden/Merrill

- Adam had a purpose for reading the article (to find more out about NCLB).
- Adam brought background knowledge to the article—he knew one of the authors and knew a lot about the legislation.
- Adam used the table of contents to find the article.
- Before reading the article, Adam skimmed it and noticed different text features.
- Adam used text features to predict the contents of the article and organize a schema.
- Adam made inferences about the contents of the article based on the photographs and text features.
- Adam questioned the bias of the author.

During this chapter, we will touch on each of these points. However, before we talk about specifics, let's address the title of this chapter, "Great Reader's Read to Learn." We purposely placed this chapter after the last chapter, "Great Readers Understand How Stories Work," because we wanted to highlight the difference between these two habits. In the last chapter, we stressed that a good story draws a reader in, encouraging us to read on to find out what happens next. In contrast, in this chapter we want to explore a different purpose for reading.

READING TO LEARN

Reading to learn involves a different purpose, and also a different type of text. Most of the time, when we read to learn, we are reading informational or nonfiction text. Some people use the terms *informational text* and *nonfiction* interchangeably; others see nonfiction text as a type of informational text. For our purposes, the label isn't important. What's most important for us is in fostering the skills and strategies a reader uses to learn from text.

Often teachers say that reading informational text is more difficult than reading stories. We don't think that's entirely true. One of the reasons many students find reading stories easier is simply because stories are more familiar to them. In the last chapter, we talked about how many of our students are surrounded by stories from the time they are babies. We described how hearing all these stories helped our students learn the structure and features of stories. Now, how many of you remember your parents reading you a bedtime newspaper article or an entry from an encyclopedia? (We're are not advocating that parents read encyclopedia articles as a bedtime ritual.) However, we are emphasizing that teachers, and parents, need to surround our students with nonfiction and narrative texts. Imagine if our students came to school as familiar with the structure of an informational book as they are with a fairy tale?

Nell Duke studied first-grade classrooms to see how much time they spent on informational text. The answer: 3.6 minutes (Duke, 2000). If we are exposing our students to informational text for less than five minutes a day, no wonder it's so hard for them to read it! From the very first day of school you should be exposing your students to informational text. Don't reserve them for the "nonfiction unit" and don't limit informational texts to your social studies and science curriculum. Given that most of what our adults read outside of school is informational (Smith, 2000) we would argue that 50% to 60% of student's reading material should be nonfiction, starting at kindergarten. We'd further argue that starting the first week of school, students should be surrounded with narrative and informational texts. You've likely noticed that previous chapters are peppered with examples using both types. Throughout the year, we model and teach using all types of texts and genres.

One simple way to share informational texts with our students is during our read-aloud and shared reading times. Often teachers shy away from reading aloud factual texts because they feel the content of the text might be too confusing, or they worry about how to share nonfiction features with their students. Thankfully, publishers and technology are helping. Publishers such as Pearson, Newbridge, National Geographic, and Rigby are creating nonfiction big books. Many schools are also buying document cameras that can project opaque objects, making it even easier to share print materials that don't come in a large format and making it possible to share other types of text including newspapers, magazine articles, and websites.

Don't misunderstand us—we aren't saying that nonfiction text doesn't present challenges for our students, challenges they wouldn't face in narrative text. Dahlia taught Adam this. Dahlia was a strong reader in Adam's fourth-grade class. During literature discussions and conferences, Dahlia came up with insightful connections and inferences. She was easily able to identify themes in class novels and thoughtfully analyzed characters. Yes, Adam thought Dahlia was one of the great readers, until it was time for her to start her animal report. Dahlia was fascinated by wolves, though she didn't know much about them. In keeping with her admirable study habits, Dahlia checked out every book in the school library on wolves—10 in all—and stuffed them into her backpack. The next day, Dahlia arrived with a note from her mother. In short, the note said that Dahlia had a difficult time making sense of her wolf books, and in frustration she threw a tantrum at home. In closing, it read, "Not a good night. We aren't sure what's wrong. Please help!"

Dahlia's problem: She didn't know to navigate nonfiction texts. As it turned out, Dahlia wasn't alone. Most of the students in Adam's class stumbled when the time came to write a research report, and it wasn't just because this was their first time doing research. Adam realized that most of his students had not had a lot of experiences in "reading to learn." In previous grades, teachers in Adam's school had taught students how to read, but they had never taught students literacy skills that would allow them to access information from texts. After a few discussions with his colleagues, Adam soon found out that his colleagues felt that this was a fourth-grade skill.

We think it's important for all teachers to understand how to teach students to read to learn. For us, teaching this habit focuses on the following elements:

1. Setting and Monitoring Your Purpose for Reading
2. Identifying and Using Text Features
3. Identifying and Using Text Structures

Setting and Monitoring Your Purpose for Reading

It's important for our students to understand the difference between fiction and nonfiction. Early in the year, especially at the primary grades, we have our students compare fiction books to nonfiction books. It's easiest to start with the books that

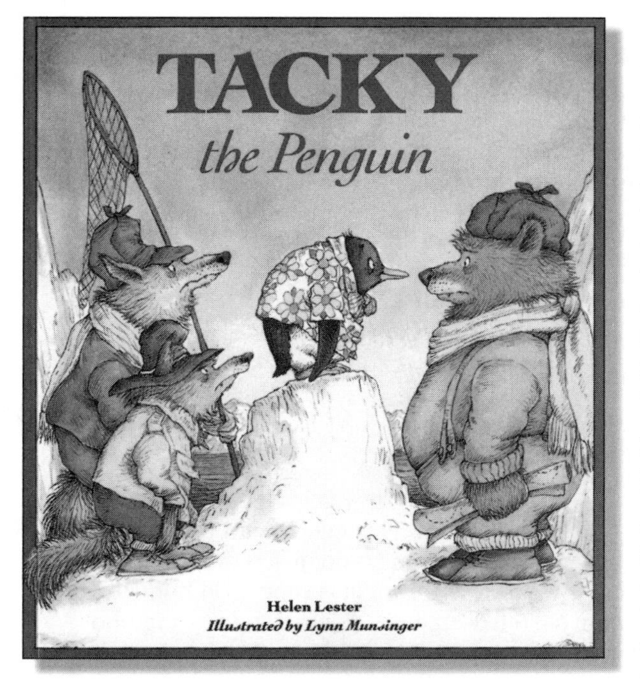

Source: Cover from *Tacky the Penguin* by Helen Lester, illustrated by Lynn Munsinger. Jacket illustrations copyright © 1988 by Lynn Munsinger. Reprinted by permission of Houghton Mifflin Company. All rights reserved.

address the same subject. For example, Doug read his students *Tacky the Penguin* (Lester, 1990) and *The Emperor's Egg* (Jenkins, 2002). After read-aloud, Doug began by asking his favorite question, "What did you notice?" After students recounted details from each of the texts, Tawnya observed, "They're different. One's true and one's not." Doug followed up with a question about the evidence she used to support her conclusion. Students quickly started to grasp the key differences between fiction and nonfiction. They started by listing the realistic-looking illustrations found in *The Emperor's Egg*, as well as the more cartoon-like features found in *Tacky the Penguin*. These students needed a bit of nudge to think about content, so Doug asked, "What did you notice the book was about?" They started to articulate that nonfiction books talk about true things and provide facts, whereas fiction deals with stories and things that are pretend or make-believe. As a follow-up, Doug used their criteria to think aloud as he sorted a small stack of books into fiction and nonfiction piles. This class convinced him that he needed to have a "both" pile for books like *The Magic School Bus* series, which contain informational text told in a narrative form.

Doug continued to move the discussion along by asking, "Why would someone read a fiction book?" and then "Why would someone read a nonfiction book?" It's important for students to understand that we read books for different purposes. Most will say you read informational books to "learn about stuff." Doug asked for examples of "stuff" they've learned from books (when there was a lull, he started to show covers of some recent read-alouds). After filling a chart, he stood back and marveled at all the information to be learned from books. He also reminded students that they "learn" from fiction as well as nonfiction.

The fact that nonfiction books contain so much information is definitely a benefit, but it's also one of the reasons why our students find this genre so challenging. You'll recall in Chapter 3 that Tia was overwhelmed by all the facts in *Exploring the Titanic* (Ballard, 1988). She was frustrated because she didn't know what the author wanted her to learn. As we discussed then, it's hard for our young readers to determine what is important because informational texts are packed with so many facts. That's why setting a purpose is so important, because purpose gives readers a focus and structures the reading experience.

Great readers set their purpose and monitor whether it is being met. You may remember from the beginning of this chapter that Adam picked up a copy of *Time* because he wanted to learn about their assessment of No Child Left Behind. He started to read with specific questions in mind, which he hoped the article would answer: Is this legislation helping schools? If so, how? How can we improve this legislation? What do experts in the field say about this legislation? We want students to approach each text with a purpose and a plan for obtaining the information they want and need to know (Purcell-Gates, Duke, Hall, & Tower, 2002).

This is how Adam taught Dahlia and the rest of his fourth-grade class to navigate through text to find the information they needed for their animal reports. Their purpose became clear once the class had determined common questions, such as:

- How does your animal communicate?
- Where does your animal live?
- What type of food does your animal eat?
- Is it a carnivore, herbivore, or omnivore?
- Is your animal nocturnal or diurnal?
- Is your animal an endangered species?

These questions guided their reading because they served as a framework for reading with purpose. Of course, we know that this is easier said than done. After his experience as Dahlia's teacher, Adam taught his students how to read for purpose more explicitly by modeling the process for a class report on honeybees. To demonstrate how readers set a purpose for reading, Adam used the big book *The Buzz About Honeybees* (Costello, 2006) to answer some specific questions. For example, Adam was searching to answer the question, "How do bees communicate?" He picked up the book and showed his class how he used the table of contents to determine whether this book addressed the question. Adam explained that the table of contents was like using a shortcut because it allowed him to zero in on the specific part of the book that would answer his question. Dahlia called out, "There's a section called, 'How do bees talk?'. I bet we'll find the answer there." Adam also modeled how he could have used the index to see if the text addressed communication. Later on in this chapter, we will talk about specific ways we can introduce our students to text features.

Source: Text Copyright © 1993 by Ann Morris. Used by permission of HarperCollins Publishers.

At the younger grades, we use picture walks to introduce reader's purpose. Nancy shows the cover of *Bread, Bread, Bread* by Ann Morris (1989) to kindergarteners. "Let's look at the cover. What type of information do you think we'll learn in this book?" Nancy purposely uses the word *information* to help focus her students and reinforce the idea that this type of text contains facts. Suggestions range from how we make bread to different types of bread and to how to eat bread. As Nancy flips through the pages, she asks students to focus on the photographs. On one page they see photographs of bagels, pita bread, and a package of white bread.

"I think I'll learn about different types of bread on this page." Nancy continues to turn the pages, modeling how she uses the photographs in order to understand the author's purpose. She encourages them to notice the details in the photographs. By the end of the picture walk, the students are brimming with questions and can't wait to read to see if the text will answer them. When the lesson is over, Nancy reflects with students on what they learned and what they still want to know about bread. She repeats this pattern many times throughout the year using informational texts of all kinds. By December her modeling has paid off. Even her nonreaders can *read* the photographs in nonfiction books to learn new information.

Of course, we don't want our students to think that the only time we pick up a nonfiction book is when we want to answer a specific question. We want our students to understand that sometimes our purpose is to learn new things, and not to answer a specific question. When you are reading nonfiction text just for fun, any information you learn is a bonus.

Identifying and Using Text Features

Photographs, diagrams, charts, maps, tables, and glossaries—today's nonfiction books are packed with numerous text features. Back in the 1980s, Adam worked at a nonfiction children's publishing company. At the time, the prevailing notion in the children's publishing industry was that young readers couldn't handle too many text features. Therefore, in addition to text, the books Adam worked on contained mostly photographs. Only a few contained glossaries, an index, or complex diagrams. Adam eventually left publishing to teach, just about the time in the 1990s when research on nonfiction text in the classroom was growing. In 1996, Adam returned to educational publishing to join *Time for Kids* as its first Education Editor. One of his primary responsibilities was to make sure that the magazine met the needs and interests of classroom teachers and elementary school students. Adam noticed the dramatic shift in what constituted quality nonfiction for kids. In each issue, the magazine staff purposely searched for ways to add complex nonfiction features to their stories. Our point here is not to show how old Adam is, but rather to emphasize how sophisticated children's nonfiction is these days. If you compare children's magazines and books to those of 20 years ago, you'll see a tremendous difference. Figure 6.1 provides a list of common nonfiction features.

After we model and show our students that informational books often contain more than just text, we send them off on scavenger hunts. We surround them with books and they chart all the features they find. At first, our wall chart contains only two columns: name of feature and where we found it. However, as our students understand text features, we add a column labeled, "what we learned." Nancy goes one step further and asks her students to create their own wall-sized text features. Her classroom walls are covered with diagrams of the parts of a caterpillar, a timeline of the life of Martin Luther King Jr., a bar chart that lists the leading home-run kings, and a topographical map of the San Diego area.

Noticing the Interactions between Features and Text

Part of modeling how to read text features includes teaching students the relationship between features and words. The interaction between images with text should

FIGURE 6.1 Organizational Features

Headings
Usually found at the top of the page or paragraph; usually printed in a larger or colored font; describes the topic or paragraph in a one- or two-word phrase; font can be different styles or sizes; used to highlight important or key information; adds variety to the page
Sidebars
Boxed information on the side of the page; usually has a border or colored background; often provides text or illustrations that add to the information in the main text
Borders
Designs or lines of color that surround the two-page spread; adds visual appeal and often fits the topic; backgrounds may be blocks of color or illustrations behind the text or photographs; adds visual appeal and usually supports the text
Captions
One to two sentences that describe an illustration or photograph; usually appears underneath the picture, but sometimes above or to the side of it
Labels
Often added to photographs or illustrations to provide more information to the reader
Diagrams, Charts, Graphs, Tables
Used to show written or additional information in a different and simple way; provides visual appeal to a two-page spread
Did You Know Facts
One to two sentences that provide a hook to the two-page spread; usually provides interesting or fascinating facts that will grab the reader's attention
Photographs and Illustrations
Adds visual appeal to the page; provides support for the written text

Source: Copyright 2004 IRA/NCTE. Read*Writer*Think. Used with permission.

support the reader's understanding (Kumpf, 2000). Many beginning readers pass over text features and just read the text. So we are explicit in explaining that great readers read the text and the features. We also need to teach our students to look for the relationship between the text and the feature. Some features work with the text to explain a concept, while others provide additional information that is not included in the text. For example, great readers look for relationships between captions and photographs and use photographs to gain a more in-depth understanding about a concept. We teach our youngest students to pay attention to the photographs by taking a book rich with photographs and masking the photographs. We then read the book using just the printed text. Then we uncover the photographs and reread. Students readily tell us how much more they learned by reading the text and the pictures.

The good news is that it's easy to find lots of examples of text features to share with students. Classroom magazines such as *National Geographic Explorer* and *Time for Kids* are great resources for exploring text features because some features echo information, while others augment. Using a think-aloud technique, Nancy illustrates to her students the ways she notices when a diagram displays information discussed directly in the main part of the text by underlining the sentences that are associated with the feature. Likewise, when she encounters a graph or chart with new information not discussed in the text, she labels it "new" to remind herself to study it closely.

It's also important for students to recognize that some informational texts are not intended to be read from beginning to end, but rather are dipped into by the reader. Magazines, newspapers, encyclopedias, and other reference books are excellent sources to use to model these lessons. Nancy likes to bring in the newspaper and tells her students that the first place she goes is to the sports section (especially during the college football season). For Adam, it's the movie section. We show them how we locate our favorite sections using the text features utilized by the newspaper editors.

Using Text Features as a Writer

To assist readers with this purpose, authors provide features that help us access the texts (see Figure 6.2). Often we introduce these features by using the analogy of guideposts. We ask our students to think about a time when they were driving with their family in an unfamiliar place. How did the driver know he or she was headed in the right direction? How did the driver get back on course when lost? They will tell us that the driver (and sometimes the passengers) look for signs. We explain that informational texts also have signs to tell you where to go. Authors know that when you pick up their books, you are often looking for something, and so you need direction to help you know where to go. Access features assist the reader in locating and organizing information quickly. For example, color is used to draw attention to key concepts, as when headings appear in blue and subheadings in red. Other access features such as the index, table of contents, and page numbers guide the reader to the exact location of a topic.

Many teachers we know ask students to create their own text features. In Chatham, New Jersey, Dawn Kurlak has her second-graders write captions for pictures she gives them. They also draw informational pictures and write their own captions. When she teaches labels, she asks each student to draw a picture of his or her face and to label at least five parts. By turning our students into creators of text

FIGURE 6.2 Access Features

Appendices	Highlighted and bolded words
Afterword, epilogue, endnotes	Index
Bibliographies	Inset sections or pages
Bulleted information	Introduction, preface, prologue
Color	Pronunciation guides
Font	Sidebars
Glossaries	Table of contents
Headings and subheadings	Title

features, we invite them to think about how and why authors chose to use different text features. For example, when we come across a diagram in a book, we challenge our students to consider why the author chose to use a diagram instead of explaining the information in a paragraph. Similarly, we encourage students to consider why an author would use a line graph instead of a bar chart. When they create their own diagrams and charts, our students finally understand how authors use these features to summarize more complicated text, making it easy for their readers to identify key ideas, relationships, and vocabulary.

By now you've read six chapters in this book. Were you able to predict some features that you'd find in this chapter? How did you expect the chapter to be organized? Did you notice how we used subheads? As authors, we put a lot of thought into how we wanted to structure this book for our readers. One of our main goals was to make sure the text was easy to understand and to follow. We purposely used elements such as titles, subheadings, and photographs to create a consistent structure for our readers. Hopefully it worked!

Identifying and Using Text Structures

In addition to features, conceptual structures are signals to the reader. When a reader sees words or phrases such as *for example*, *in summary*, and *in conclusion*, they know something is happening—an explication, a review, or a signal that the reading will end soon. In college, we used to pull out a highlighter every time we saw one of these words. Nancy tells her students that these are "Stop and Think" words and keeps a running list in the classroom.

Luckily this approach to writing isn't unique. Most children's writers are conscious of the organizational text structures that make concepts more coherent. These structures include:

- Description/Exemplification (Concept/Definition)
- Compare/Contrast
- Cause and Effect
- Problem/Solution
- Temporal/Chronological/Sequential

However, not all of our students know how to identify these structures, and even if they can identify them, they don't know how to use them to make sense of what they are reading. Research shows that understanding how a text is organized helps readers construct meaning and promotes recall (Wolfe, 2005).

These text structures can often be identified by their use of signal words—words or phrases used in the text to alert the reader to know how the information is being organized. Good readers use knowledge of structure and signal words more effectively than struggling readers (Kletzien, 1992). Figure 6.3 shows the relationship between types of informational texts and the signal words most closely associated with them.

Description/exemplification. This type of text describes people, places, or phenomena. Nearly all informational books have passages that are descriptive. Signal

FIGURE 6.3 Signal Words in Expository Texts

Text Structure	Purpose	Signal Words
Exemplification	Describes people, places, or phenomena	Descriptive adjectives, adverbs, and phrases For example For instance
Compare and contrast	Explains how two or more people, places, or phenomena are alike or different	Although Compared to However In comparison Like/unlike Same/different Similar to Whereas While yet
Cause and effect	Shows causal relationship	As a result Because If . . . then In order to Since So So that Therefore
Problem and solution	Describes problems and solutions	Accordingly Answer Decide Question Problem Thus
Temporal or sequential	Chronological order	Afterwards Another Before Finally First In addition Last Next Second Then Third

Source: Frey, N., & Fisher, D. (2006). *Language art workshop: Purposeful reading and writing instruction* (p. 339). Upper Saddle River, NJ: Pearson/Merrill/Prentice Hall. Used with permission.

words for exemplification text structure include descriptive adjectives, adverbs, and phrases. For instance, a passage about ancient Egypt wouldn't label the mummy merely as *old*, but would offer a richer description that explains that the mummy is "wrapped in discolored linen bandages wound tightly around the entire body, lying undisturbed for thousands of years deep in the cool, dark, mud brick pyramid."

Compare/contrast. Text structures that compare and contrast use descriptive language, but also explain how two or more people, places, or phenomena are similar or different. Like exemplification, most textbooks contain some compare/contrast passages as well. Signal words such as *although*, *yet*, *while*, *however*, *something/different*, *like/unlike*, and other words that show opposites are likely to appear. "*Although* the first mummies were probably accidental, mummification became an art in ancient Egypt. *While* members of the noble classes were mummified, poor people usually were not."

Cause and effect. These text structures, which show causal relationships between phenomena, can be deceptively similar to compare/contrast, but their signal words give them away. Words such as *since*, *because*, *as a result*, and *if . . . then* statements are frequently seen in these passages. "*Because* the Incas lived in the high Andes, they created ice mummies that were preserved in the thin, frigid mountain air."

Problem/solution. Another text structure is problem/solution. Seen frequently in mathematics textbooks, they contain signal words such as *questions*, *answer*, *thus*, *accordingly*, and *decide*. A challenge of problem/solution is that it is more subtle than some of the others and may develop over the course of several sentences or paragraphs. "Theft and the desert climate have taken their toll on Egyptian mummies. *Accordingly*, the government has taken steps to preserve the remaining mummies by installing climate-controlled displays and sophisticated security devices."

Temporal/chronological/sequential. More easy to detect is our final text structure, the sequential or temporal (time-based) passage. These signal words jump out of the text for most readers and include words such as *first*, *next*, *last*, *before*, *afterwards*, *another*, and *finally*. (If you were paying attention to the structure of this sequential paragraph, you knew we were coming to the end by the use of the word *finally*.) "The *first* step in the mummification process was to remove all the internal organs. *Next*, the embalmer drained the body of fluids. *Finally*, the body was wrapped in linens" (Frey & Fisher, 2006, pp. 338, 340).

Thinking Aloud with Text Structures

As we read aloud, we stop when we come to these organizational structures and signal words and point them out for our students. When Doug reads aloud the first page of Diane Stanley's (2003) wonderful picture book *Michelangelo* to fifth-graders, he discusses the way the author establishes a sense of the passage of time leading up to the birth of the great artist. Poverty has haunted the family "for the past few generations" and a date is established: "1474." "Late in the autumn of that year" his parents move to another town in search of financial stability "on a journey of several days."

Michelangelo's birth comes "in the early morning hours of March 6, 1475" (p. 1). Doug thinks aloud, "It seems like the author wanted to make sure that I understood when this happened, that it was a long time ago. But she also wants to remind me that a long time ago isn't just one event. She shows how time unfolds for this family—they had been poor a long time, and had grown up that way. They went on a journey that wasn't easy, especially for a pregnant woman. And then the author ends the passage with an important fact—the birth date of the artist."

Uncovering Text Structures in Reading

Students need opportunities to locate the structures embedded in their readings. Ideally, we would like them to mark up the books, but this isn't practical. Newspapers are a great resource for this purpose. Armed with highlighters (already you have their attention), they work together to locate signal words that reveal text structures. It can be overwhelming to give them an entire newspaper to sort through, so we clip articles in advance, screening them for content and interest, and then distribute four or five to each group. The choice to pair students is a deliberate one, because it gives us the opportunity to listen in to their thinking processes as they locate text structures. When we see students racing ahead to scan for signal words before reading the article, we remind them that their task isn't merely to complete a scavenger hunt for words, but to understand how the signal words relate to text structure, which in turn speak to the concepts in the story. After reviewing the articles and highlighting signal words, the partners glue them into their notebooks and compose an explanation of the structure and the way the author used it to convey the information in the story.

This task is too complex for younger students, so we use our school's poster maker (a heat transfer duplicator that enlarges print materials). Nancy hangs the enlarged passage on the easel and reads it to and with her students, and then they discuss the ideas the author is sharing. They look for the sequential words like *first*, *next*, and *last* in simple passages Nancy writes to explain how pancakes are made or how to plant a seed. She encourages students to use similar signal words in their own writing to explain a process. Their writing is assembled into a class "how-to" book that includes topics as diverse as "How to Play Twister" and "How to Make a Peanut Butter and Jelly Sandwich."

Our goal is to help our students understand that they should be looking for these text structures as they read. As a reminder, Doug has students create bookmarks with the following questions:

- How do I think the information is organized?
- How is the information chunked?
- Am I finding other structures embedded in the text?

When we conference with students or work with them in guided reading groups, we continue to ask and emphasize these questions. We ask our students to incorporate these structures into their own writing, often with the aid of a graphic organizer. Laying out ideas in a visual display seems to work well for many students, who find this less tedious than writing lists or notes. Although graphic organizers can and should be used flexibility, we have discovered that the following pairings work particularly well.

- Description/exemplification: semantic maps
- Compare/contrast: Venn diagrams

- Cause/effect: T-charts, fishbone maps
- Problem/solution: decision trees
- Sequential/chronological/temporal: flowcharts, chain of event maps

Graphic organizers are intended to be an intermediate step to something else, written or verbal. We don't want to reinforce the false notion that they are an end product unto themselves. Therefore, pairing graphic organizers with text structures is effective for introducing their purposes. We'll discuss the teaching and use of graphic organizers in more detail in the next chapter. However, it is a reminder to us about the interaction between and among habits: They don't stand in isolation of one another. Each habit informs another.

MOVING FROM GOOD TO GREAT

There has been a growing appreciation in this decade for the importance of informational texts in elementary and middle school. Educators recognize the need for exposure to these rich resources, and the flood of this genre into classrooms encourages us. However, exposure alone isn't enough. The "fourth-grade slump" has been well documented over the years (Chall, Jacobs, & Baldwin, 1990), and classroom teachers have always known that the shift from "learning to read" to "reading to learn" leaves some children gasping for air. Beyond exposure from the earliest grades, readers need to acquire the habits associated with reading nonfiction texts. This means that they purposefully shift their attention to accommodate their purposes and monitor the degree to which they understand what they read. As with other genres, great readers formulate questions and seek other sources to expand and clarify their understanding of the topic. Great readers are adept at utilizing the features unique to informational books and articles and synthesize the content presented in those features with what is being presented in the main body of the text. They also recognize the relationship between the conceptual frameworks utilized by the author and the way he or she structures the writing to make those concepts clear. This is a tall order for readers, and one that demands that we continually return to and expand upon their ability to do this. Our classrooms are drenched in vibrant informational texts, but it is our job to make those texts come alive and to habituate our students to the ways in which we comprehend them.

Does the student:

Set and Monitor the Purpose for Reading

- Identify a purpose for reading?
- Preview a nonfiction book to see if it matches his or her purpose for reading?
- Form questions based on the purpose for reading that are appropriate for the text?
- Scan the text to answer questions and locate specific information?

- Identify the author's purpose?
- Identify characteristics of a nonfiction text?
- Use knowledge of a topic to ask questions he or she hopes the text will answer?
- Use the text to learn new information?
- Use the photographs to learn new information?
- Use what he or she learned to generate new questions about the topic?

Identify and Use Text Features

- Tell what an index is, and use it to find specific information?
- Explain how words in a glossary are organized, and use the glossary to determine the meaning of words?
- Recognize a sidebar?
- Read visual information from maps, diagrams, charts, table, graphs, and timelines?
- Use visual information to help understand concepts discussed in the text?
- Distinguish between a photograph and illustration?
- Understand why authors use direct quotes?
- Differentiate between text features and text structure?

Identify and Use Text Structures

- Recognize time-order text structure?
- Recognize description text structure?
- Recognize problem/solution text structure?
- Recognize comparison/contrast text structure?
- Recognize cause/effect text structure?

Professional Development

1. Develop a partnership with a local newspaper or magazine. Brainstorm some possible projects. For example, a student paper or magazine. Ask writers and editors to discuss how, and why, they incorporate text structures and text features in their stories.
2. Create a parent newsletter that features tips and suggestions for nonfiction read-alouds. A good place for resources is the International Reading Association website (www.reading.org).
3. Devote a faculty meeting to compare how your students comprehend fiction versus nonfiction text. A great starting place is a retelling inventory, the Developmental Reading Assessment (DRA), or similar formative reading assessments.
4. Invite your students to create authentic nonfiction resources for your school. For example, they could write informed pieces for a student handbook on topics such as "Finding your way around the school," "Checking out books from the library," "Fun games to play at recess," or "What to expect in first grade" (second grade, etc.).

References

Ballard, R. D. (1988). *Exploring the Titanic.* New York: Scholastic.

Chall, J. S., Jacobs, V. A., & Baldwin, L. E. (1990). *The reading crisis: Why poor child fall behind.* Cambridge, MA: Harvard University Press.

Costello, E. (2006). *The buzz about honeybees.* Parsippany: NJ: Pearson Education.

Duke, N. K. (2000). 3.6 minutes per day: The scarcity of informational texts in first grade. *Reading Research Quarterly, 35*, 202–224.

Frey, N., & Fisher, D. (2006). *Language arts workshop: Purposeful reading and writing instruction.* Upper Saddle River: NJ: Pearson Prentice Hall Merrill.

Jenkins, M. (2002). *The emperor's egg.* Cambridge, MA: Candlewick.

Kletzien, S. B. (1992). Proficient and less proficient comprehenders' strategy for different top-level structures. *Journal of Reading Behavior, 24*, 191–215.

Kumpf, E. P. (2000). Visual discourse: Designing the considerate text. *Technical Communication Quarterly, 9*, 401–424.

Lester, H. (1990). *Tacky the penguin.* New York: Houghton Mifflin.

Morris, A. (1989). *Bread, bread, bread.* New York: Lothrop, Lee, & Shepard.

Purcell-Gates, V., Duke, N. K., Hall, L., & Tower, C. (2002, December). *Text purposes and text use: A case from elementary science instruction.* Paper presented at the annual meeting of the National Reading Conference, Miami, FL.

Smith, M. C. (2000). The real-world reading of adults. *Journal of Literacy Research, 32*, 25–32.

Stanley, D. (2003). *Michelangelo.* New York: Harper Trophy.

Wolfe, M. B. W. (2005). Memory for narrative and expository text: Independent influences of semantic associations and text organization. *Journal of Experimental Psychology: Learning, Memory, and Cognition, 31*, 359–364.

CHAPTER 7

Great Readers Monitor and Organize What They Read

Several years ago, Adam's boss told him that his desk was a mess AND that in general he was disorganized. She recommended that he first try a self-help book; if that didn't work, take a course; and if that didn't work, well there's the door. Adam spent hours at the local bookstore browsing through shelves of books on getting organized. "At least I'm not alone," he thought, "there must be lots of disorganized people in the world." The advice he found ranged from "only touch a piece of paper once" to faithfully using a daily planner to developing the habits of highly effective people (sound familiar?). A quick look at a used bookstore might suggest that we either quickly master these skills or abandon the effort, as there is shelf after shelf of these books.

Why is organization such an important aspect of reading, not to mention life? Yes, we're busy and being busy makes us forget things. But it's more than that. Being organized facilitates getting things done. Knowing where your car keys are, for example, reduces the amount of time you spend in the morning looking for them. It's that simple. The bottom line for Adam was that his boss thought he wasn't efficient.

Interestingly, we each have ways of being organized. Some of these systems are more or less helpful. Nancy likes piles; there are piles all around her workspace organized (sometimes) by priority of what needs to be done when. Doug likes folders and has a folder for everything from the next conference he's going to attend to the things that he wants to buy. Adam, well, he's still searching for a system that works for him.

As Marcus Aurelius, the Roman emperor, noted, "The secret of all victory lies in the organization of the non-obvious." We couldn't agree more. Being a great reader requires organization of thinking, organization of information, and organizational systems. Great readers understand the non-obvious: reading as an act of cognitive organization. Austin really taught Doug this. Anytime he wanted to have a reader's conference with him, Austin would gather his book and his notes, ready to engage us in conversations about Egyptians. Austin organized his thinking into

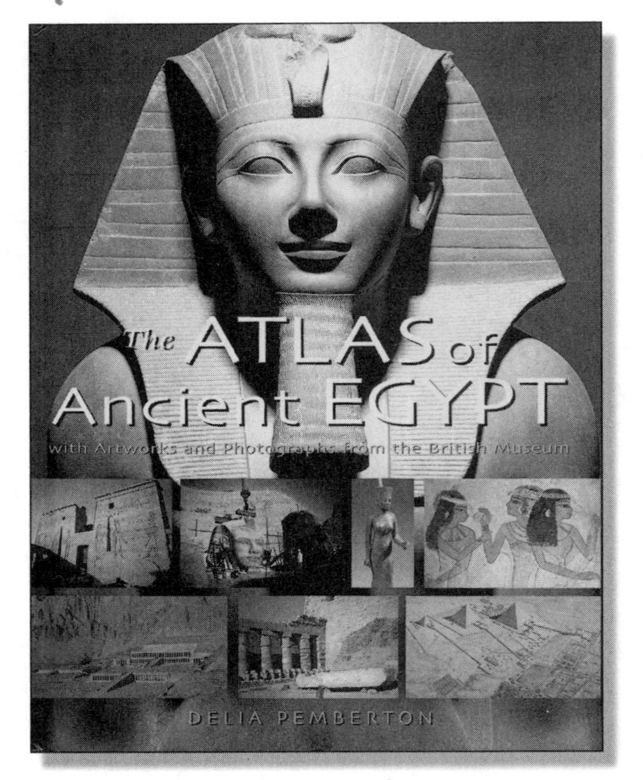

Source: Book cover from Pemberton, D. (2005). *The atlas of ancient Egypt.* New York: Harry N. Abrams.

categories that helped him remember things. He also had a list of questions that he still needed to figure out. Doug recalled one particular conversation during the time Austin was reading *Egyptology* (Ward, Andrew, & Steer, 2004), a fascinating book with pop-up pages and supplemental content such as "mummy cloth."

During the conversation, Austin talked a great deal about the layers used when preparing a body for mummification. Austin had notes about the process written in his journal and could explain this process. He also said that he was confused by part of the book. In his words, "I'm not sure about the lost tomb of Osiris. I never heard of that before, so maybe it's just fantasy. That's my next question; I have to find out if this part is true or make-believe." He selected a reading from the book *The Atlas of Ancient Egypt* (Pemberton, 2005) to read to find out the answer to his next question.

See, Austin was able to use his notes in an authentic way. He also monitored his comprehension, comparing what he already read to the information in the current book he was reading. He was able to refer back to his notes to find out if he knew anything about the lost tomb of Osiris, which he did not. Unfortunately, there are too many cases in which students are provided with instruction in organizational skills for the sake of tidiness, and not learning. In these cases, students spend considerable amounts of time and attention focused on the organizational system, and not on the content. Yes, it's important for our students to have a clean desk, a neat cubby, and tabs in their notebook. But it is also important that they attend to the ways in which ideas and concepts are organized, both in their heads and in their notes and materials.

MONITORING AND ORGANIZING WHAT IS READ

A long time ago, Laura Ingalls Wilder, famed children's author of *Little House on the Prairie*, suggested, "The trouble with organizing a thing is that pretty soon folks get to paying more attention to the organization than to what they're organized for." As we explore this habit, monitoring and organizing ideas and information, let's make sure that we pay attention to this perspective. For us, it's yet another example of the difference between good (or good enough) readers and great readers. Good enough readers display systems for their teachers; great readers use these systems to learn while reading.

External Systems for Monitoring and Organizing

As students learn how to read, they learn to track information and hold it in their short- and long-term memories. One method for developing this ability is to show children how effective readers make notes about the text. This is accomplished through the use of language charts, sticky notes, summary frames, and graphic organizers. We touched on some of these methods in Chapter 3, when we talked about Tia, the student who could recall isolated facts about the *HMS Titanic*, but had difficulty synthesizing ideas into a meaningful whole. In her case, pausing to complete notes helped her to keep a focus on how the facts related to one another. This organizational tool served as a way for Tia to monitor her understanding. The ability to create notes in a variety of forms, including on graphic organizers and in journals, allows students to sort out their ideas in a cohesive fashion. Karen Bromley observed that "organizers show important ideas and information and relationships among concepts in texts" (1999, p. 169). These displays of visual information also serve as manifestations to our students, and us, that they understand.

Internal Systems for Monitoring and Organizing

Graphic organizers and note taking are external tools that help us to organize and keep track of information. The internal strategies we use are self-monitoring and visualizing. As with external organization of ideas, these inner habits of mind serve to assemble bits of information into a meaningful whole. Marie Clay noted, "[C]hildren learn to monitor themselves to keep their correct reading on track, and when something seems to be wrong they usually search for a way to get rid of the dissonance. It is important for teachers to notice self-monitoring because the process is a general one required in all reading" (2001, p. 185). Did you stumble over the word *dissonance*, when you first read this sentence? If you paused and thought, "I wonder what Clay meant here," then you were self-monitoring. Monitoring and self-correction are a form of self-repair that all readers use to maintain understanding of the text. Great readers also have a number of fix-up strategies to use when their understanding is compromised.

Another way that students monitor and organize their reading is through the use of visualizing. We all do this; we create mental images or play movies in our minds as we read. For many of us, visualizing seems intuitive. Adam visualizes so much when he reads a well-crafted novel that he sometimes doesn't remember if he read the book or saw the movie. Building on the mental imagery addressed in previous chapters, students use illustrations, background knowledge, dialogue, and vocabulary to extend their understanding and notice when it is different from others (Borduin, Borduin, & Manley, 1994).

Great readers have both external and internal systems for monitoring and organizing what they read. We develop this habit in at least four ways, which we will describe in greater detail in the pages that follow.

1. Taking Notes on Fiction
2. Taking Notes on Nonfiction Text
3. Self-monitoring
4. Visualizing

Taking Notes on Fiction

It is important to acknowledge at the outset that taking notes on fiction differs from taking notes on nonfiction. We don't expect great readers to stop reading the newest book by their favorite author and take elaborate notes. We do expect that readers of fiction will figure out ways to take notes on important plot twists, favorite lines of dialogue, or descriptions that make their skin crawl. For example, while reading *Nineteen Minutes* (Picoult, 2007), a novel about a school shooting, Doug turned down the corner of a page and underlined a sentence that he wanted to talk about further. The line read, "If you gave someone your heart and they died, did they take it with them?" (p. 102). Doug made connections between the character in the book who lost her boyfriend and loss of loved ones in general. In the margin, Doug wrote himself a note to talk about this question in juxtaposition with the perspective of Joan Didion (2005) who wrote about the sudden loss of her husband in *The Year of Magical Thinking*.

On a lighter but related note, Nancy was working with a group of five fourth-grade struggling readers who had selected the book *Charlotte's Web* (White, 1952) for their book club. (Don't worry, these weren't the inner-city kids from Chapter 4; they had appropriate background knowledge.) After completing each chapter, members of the group constructed a poster-sized concept map of the main points in the chapter. These charts helped the students to keep track of important points, focus on the characters, and make predictions. They often referred to their notes, super-sized as they were, during discussions with Nancy. At one point, with tissue in hand, Nancy and this group of students discussed the impending death of Charlotte. As Joe said, "I knew it, I knew it. She's gonna die. Wilbur can't save her. Remember when she helped Wilbur when he thought he was going to be Christmas dinner?" Joe flipped through the pages to find the notes on Chapter 7. "The old sheep told Wilbur he was getting fattened up for dinner, and Charlotte told him she would save him." Joe not only recognized the foreshadowing, he also knew when it had occurred in the story because the visual representation of the notes made it easy for Joe to locate the information he was seeking.

The hallmark, or litmus test, for a successful fiction note-taking strategy is to help students ask the question: Does this information matter? Fiction writers provide a great deal of detail that students don't need to have in their notes. The key, then, is to ensure that students focus on things that matter while taking notes on fiction. Early in the year, we introduce note taking as an aid to retelling and summarizing. Then, we are teaching note taking simply as a vehicle to remembering information. When we return to note taking later in the year, we show students how notes can help us understand a story. For example, we talk about how we can use notes to help us pay attention to character development. As Nancy Roser and her colleagues (2005) demonstrated, stories contain lessons that characters learn and grow from. By focusing on characters, the reader can also consider the setting, conflicts, dialogue, and plot changes. As Emery (1996) suggested, understanding characters—their desires, feelings, thoughts, hopes, dreams, fears, and beliefs—lies at the very heart of literary meaning making. This perspective is furthered by Anthony Burgess, a novelist who was well known for his book *A Clockwork Orange* (1962). He said, "There is not much point in writing a novel unless you can show the possibility of moral transformation, or an increase in wisdom, operating in your chief character or characters."

Bruce Laurance/Getty Images, Inc. Photodisc

As the students in Nancy's class learned, graphic organizers are a helpful way for organizing notes about characters while reading fiction. The Read*Write*Think website operated by the International Reading Association and the National Council of Teachers of English provides an interactive story map that students can use to organize their thinking about characters. It can be found at: www.readwritethink.org/materials/storymap.

In addition, there are a number of excellent graphic organizers in Jim Burke's (2002) book, *Tools for Thought: Graphic Organizers for Your Classroom.* You'll find a number of interactive graphic organizers, which we will discuss further in the section that follows this, on Dinah Zike's website (www.dinah.com). We like these because they are interactive and students can manipulate the paper while they are thinking. Finally, there are a number of free graphic organizers available from EdHelper (www.edhelper.com).

Importantly, the graphic organizer should not be the end product. Graphic organizers should be used to organize information and monitor understanding. Students should do something with the graphic organizers, such as retell, summarize, discuss, debate, or write an essay. The important thing is that the graphic organizer is seen as a tool and not the final product. As readers gain more experience with using graphic organizers, they should be the ones determining when a Venn diagram suits their purposes because there's a lot of comparing and contrasting going on, or if a story map is the best way to keep track of the elements because they are going to turn the text into a Reader's Theater script. Great readers have tools that they intentionally use; they don't just complete worksheets.

Taking Notes on Nonfiction Text

Is note taking simply a school behavior? We know that it's useful in education, especially in college, but do people in the "real world" take notes? Nancy's son, Eric, is a manufacturing engineer who works for a company that manufactures valves. His specific job, which Nancy notes that he is particularly well suited for, is to break the valves and study how they break. (Nancy never thought his talent for breaking things would ever lead to a career.) Of course, he's paid to improve the valves so that they don't break on customers. And guess what? He takes notes on the process, he takes notes when he visits customers who have broken valves, and he takes notes when he's reading from informational texts about *stress points*, *corrosion*, *breakaway couplings*, and *poppets*. A look through Eric's notes exemplifies how note taking is a habit that great readers use well into their professional lives.

As we have noted, taking notes on nonfiction differs in important ways from taking notes on fiction. Nonfiction texts are read to find things out, to learn, and to answer questions we have. As such, notes help us remember the information and to find the information again later. There are a number of systems we use to take notes while reading for information. The most common note-taking page is probably the Cornell note page (Pauk, 1974). A typically Cornell note page is divided into three areas: a minor column on the left, a major column on the right, and a space for a summary at the bottom. We have used this type of note-taking tool with students from grades K–12 (e.g., Frey & Fisher, 2007; Fisher & Frey, 2008). Jordan, a seventh-grader, developed a note-taking page based on his reading of *Phineas Gage: A Gruesome but True Story About Brain Science* (Fleishman, 2002) which can be found in Figure 7.1. You'll notice that Jordan uses a Cornell note page to organize his thinking. You'll also notice that he references pages from the book so that he can return to the text when he wants to.

Introducing Note Taking

When teaching very young children, note taking is modeled by the teacher, who creates notes during shared reading and writing times. Using a large piece of chart paper, the teacher sets up a simple note-taking page and writes key ideas down during the reading. How-to books that explain processes are ideal for this purpose. Nancy read the book *How to Be a Friend* (Brown & Brown, 2001) to first-grade students and modeled note taking on the second reading. She made a list of the sections from the table of contents in the minor column, using headings such as "Bosses and Bullies" and "How to Make Up With a Friend." As they reread the book, she and the students noticed important ideas, and she wrote them in the major column. For example, she wrote "protect a friend if someone is bothering him" after Justin identified it as an important idea from the book. The following day, Nancy reviewed the notes with the class and told them that she tries to write one or two sentences that explain the most important ideas of the book. She said, "Friends take care of each other, even when it is hard. They work at being friends." She wrote this in the summary section and hung the completed note page in the writing center. Later, students composed a paragraph of their own, using the ideas from the notes.

FIGURE 7.1 Sample Note-taking Page

Big Ideas	Details
1. Who was Phineas?	1. railroad worker in 18 2. He had an accident in 1848 3. He lived until 1860
2. Why was he famous?	1. A railroad tamping rod went through his skull 2. He lived, but had brain damage 3. His personality changed
What was damaged?	1. frontal lobe → 2. It missed his optical nerve so he could still see
What effects?	1. The frontal cortez messed up so his behavior was changed. 2. Thrown out of towns 3. Lied, tricked people, mean 4. He wasn't that way before accident
What was learned by science?	1. Frontal lobe controls behavior 2. parts of brain have different jobs 3. You have to operate on brains carefully or you can ruin a person's life.
Summary:	Phineas Gage had a rod go through his head in 1848. He lived but his personality changed and he died miserable. The frontal cortex was damaged and scientist learned about the brain.

Connecting Note Taking to Other Knowledge

In addition to generic note-taking systems such as Cornell notes, great readers of informational texts understand that authors use specific text structures. A working knowledge of these text structures helps readers to organize their thinking and to remember the information (Armbruster, Anderson, & Ostertag, 1987). You'll recall that Chapter 6 contains a list of common text structures, with examples and the signal words readers use to notice the structures. These structures also assist students in creating useful notes that can aid in their understanding of text.

It's easy to see why this helps the great reader. While reading from her third-grade science text, Avani noticed that the author had identified a problem. In the book, the author described living things that caused changes in the environment in which they lived, but the example focused on light pollution and its impact on animals. In her notes, she listed the problem, knowing full well that the author would describe the solution. Avani's teacher had focused her instruction on text structures as an organizing system. She taught the class to notice text structures through signal words. She also focused on the content or what to write down. For problem/solution texts, the students learned to focus on:

- *Problems:* could be something terrible or a situation that someone wants changed
- *Actions:* what is being done to address the problem
- *Results:* what is the result of the action in attempting to address the problem

By internalizing information about text structures, Avani was about to focus on the content of the text and determine what the author was trying to tell her. She had a system for organizing this information, which in turn helped her to remember it.

Another way to take notes about informational texts comes from our dear friend Dinah Zike and her work on Foldables™. These interactive graphic organizers allow students to manipulate and organize information. Dinah has organized Foldables based on a number of thinking processes, such as comparing and contrasting, as well as on organizational systems such as processes. For example, Jacob was taking notes on the differences between carnivores, herbivores, and omnivores. As can be seen in Figure 7.2, he used a Venn diagram on a folded piece of paper to organize his information for later use. Jacob didn't stop his collection of information about this topic after reading one piece of text. Given that he had an organizational system, he added to it as he learned more about these three words. Again, information about interactive graphic organizers, Foldables, can be found at www.dinah.com.

Regardless of the method of note taking, relevance is key. Make sure that your students see authentic examples of ways that you, and others, use note taking in the real world. Invite the principal, the custodian, and a cafeteria worker to share their notes. The more examples, the better.

Self-monitoring

Thinking about how well a reading task is progressing is a critical component of reading comprehension. You do it and we do it. Great readers know how to monitor their understanding of what they are reading, and they do so as they read. Of course it's an invisible process, one that readers do in their minds. However, you can see the outward behavior of self-monitoring as readers reread, ask questions, sequence information, and talk about their reading with others. As Glazer (1992) notes, we can teach students to self-monitor through think-alouds, feedback, and practice.

FIGURE 7.2 Sample Foldable™

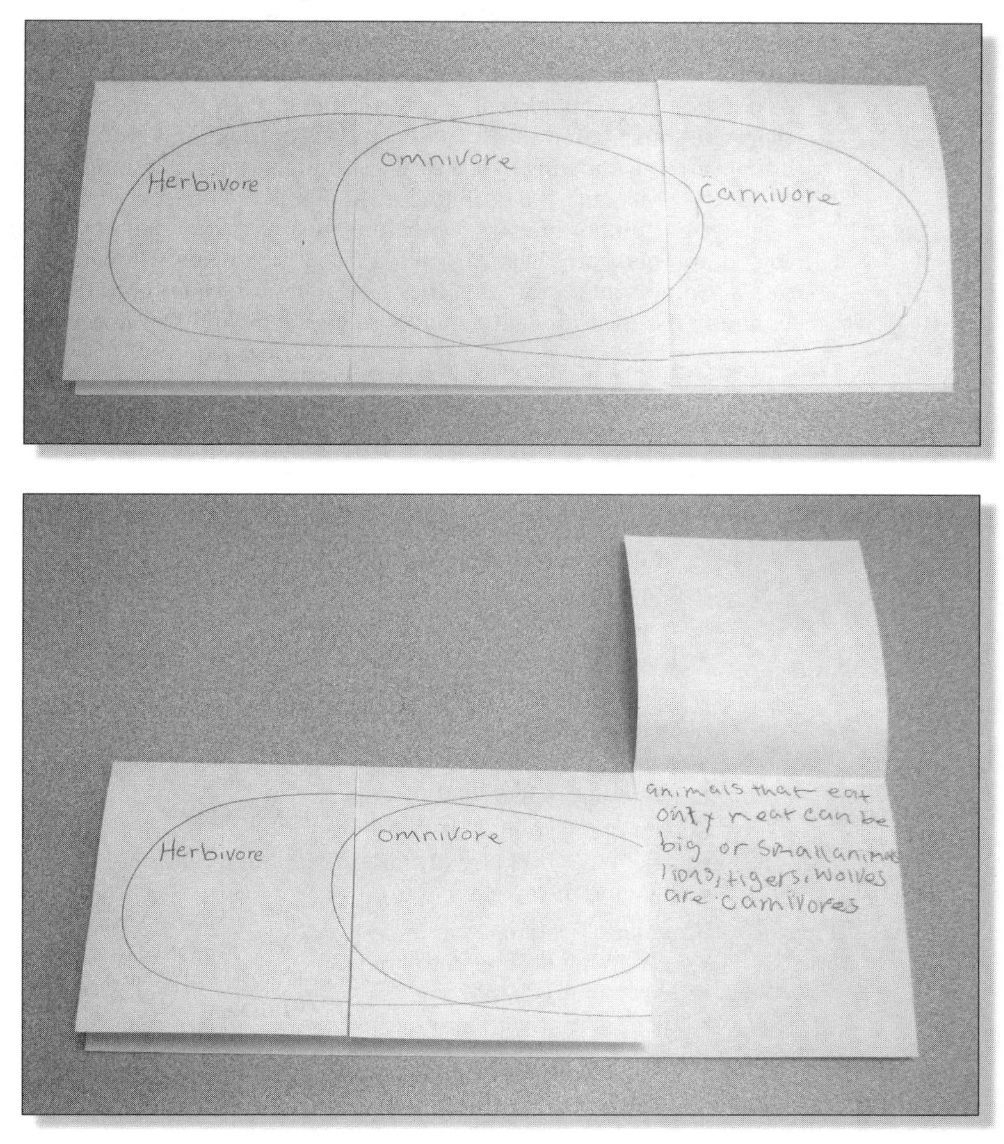

Our experience suggests that self-monitoring isn't the problem. Students know when they don't understand. The issue is more often that either they don't care if the book doesn't make sense or they don't know what to do if it doesn't make sense. For those who don't care, who aren't motivated or engaged, the intervention is straightforward. They need to choose something to read and to have someone talk about their choice with them. We have yet to find a student who couldn't self-monitor in books he or she selected, especially when the student in question knows that he or she will engage in a number of conversations about the text with one of us.

That brings us to students who don't know what to do when they self-monitor and realize that they don't have a clue about what they've read. The intervention for these students is a bit more complex. As Richard Allington (2002) taught us, "you can't learn from books you can't read" (p. 16). So the first question we ask students is whether or not the selected book is simply too difficult. They may choose to read it for bits and pieces of information (such as the student in Chapter 4 who wanted to know more about turtles), knowing that they won't understand everything in the book.

If the book isn't too difficult and students are interested in it, then they need to be taught a number of ways for making meaning from the text. In the world of reading comprehension, these are called fix-up strategies. There are a number of them and it's important to note that they all don't work equally well at all times. The most common fix-up strategies, as outlined by Keene and Zimmermann (1997), include:

- Grapho-Phonic System
  - sound out words (beginning/ending sounds)
  - point and slide across the word
  - ask "Do the letters match the sounds?"
- Lexical System
  - look for clues in surrounding text
  - look for prefixes, suffixes, root words
- Syntactic System
  - read aloud (Does it sound right?)
  - read the word faster or slower
  - exaggerate punctuation clues
- Semantic System
  - substitute another word that would make sense
  - reread or read ahead
- Schematic System
  - ask "What do I already know?" (about text/author)
  - imagine the scene
- Pragmatic System
  - ask "What do I need to know?"
  - ask "What is important?"
  - discuss text with another person

Again, the key to monitoring is to notice when you're not understanding, to care enough to do something about it, and to have a plan for returning to meaning making. It should be obvious, but we better say it. Most of the reading students do should be EASY for them. They should only have to use fix-up strategies occasionally. They should experience a great deal of teacher modeling of these strategies and have significant amounts of guided practice to get good at using them. Then, when they come into contact with confusing texts that they want to read, students will have a chance at understanding.

As you read, model the ways in which you monitor your understanding. Nancy likes to use a strategy developed by Sharon Vaughn and Janette Klingner (1999) called "Clicks and Clunks" to model how a reader notices a loss of meaning and then fixes it. Using the analogy of a metal detector, she explains that reading is mostly about the "clicks"—as the words and ideas make sense, your understanding hums along at a good pace, and the meaning "clicks" in your head. However, just like a metal detector locating something unseen, meaning can be disrupted by the "clunk" of an unknown word, a confusing idea, or the loss of connection to previous information. When the "clunk" goes off, it's time to pause to figure out what went wrong. She then models fix-up strategies like structural and contextual analysis, rereading, substituting words, and so on.

This discussion reminds Doug of reading with Cari, a precocious second-grader. Most of the texts in the classroom were easy for her to read. During a routine trip to a bookstore with her parents, Cari stumbled across *The Adventures of Captain Underpants* (Pilkey, 1997). Her parents didn't know about the controversy with this book, and probably wouldn't have cared had they known. Anyway, this book was the first book that gave Cari a run for her money. However, she was very motivated to read this book (and tell her fellow students about it). It was also the first time that she was interested in fix-up strategies, because she needed them. Cari had to reread several parts of the text to ensure her understanding. She also had to slow down her reading rate to ensure that she would remember all of the details from the story. Importantly, her strategic use of fix-up strategies did not detract from her enjoyment of the book. As Cari reported, "This is my favorite book. He first wrote it when he was in second grade, just like me. I'm going to write a book too. I also read *Georgie the Ghost* (Odorizzi, 1990) and *Harold and the Purple Crayon* (Johnson, 1955) because they were the favorite books of my favorite author." Again, as Cari reminded us, reading doesn't have to be hard, but it does need to have a purpose.

Visualizing

As we have noted, reading should almost always be easy. We tell students that they will know they're understanding a text when they see the text in their mind, like a movie or video. Years ago that may have sounded crazy, but today we think of this as visualizing. Like self-monitoring, visualizing is an invisible process. Also like self-monitoring, there are behaviors that teachers can observe that are based on visualizing. We expect students to be able to describe what they see in their mind, the visual information as well as the connections they make. We also expect students to add details—such as the time of day, seasons, feelings of characters, and such—that the author does not provide. It is this later practice that distinguishes good readers from great readers. Simply said, the author cannot provide all of the details in the text and must, instead, rely on the reader to add his or her own. Nancy and C. J. discussed this vivid passage from *Left for Dead* (Nelson, 2003) about the shark attacks on the survivors of the sinking of the *U.S.S. Indianapolis:*

> First one man screamed, then another. The sharks seemed to be attacking men who'd drifted loose from the nets. The men closed ranks. It didn't help. Men were pulled under, and their bodies bobbed to the surface, minus an appendage, only to disappear again. Twible set up shark watches, appointing men to serve as lookouts, but it didn't help much. The sharks periodically came and went, indifferent to both shouts and prayers. (pp. 69–70)

Needless to say, a visualizing exercise for this passage would be chilling and probably unnecessary. Nancy chose to ask C. J. about the thoughts and feelings of the men. She asked them to picture their faces. "They're terrified," he quietly replied. "They've never seen anything like it, not even in a nightmare." She asked him what he heard as he read that passage. "Those words, 'shouts and prayers,' that's what I heard. I was imagining some people crying for help, and also the sounds my grandma makes when she prays the rosary," he said. In this way, visualizing was used to understand, not to recall.

Unfortunately, this is not often the point of instruction. Instead, we have observed teachers requiring that students draw what the author describes or tell a partner how they "see" the author's words. For us, this is akin to basic recall, just done in a visual way. It may, in fact, disrupt reading and meaning making rather than facilitate understanding. What students need is instruction in visualizing to fill in the gaps that the author leaves for the reader.

As a word of caution, when students are taught to visualize, they like to share what they see in their minds with others. Michael was reading *The Higher Power of Lucky* (Patron, 2006), a Newbury gold winner about a 10-year-old girl named Lucky who entertains herself by eavesdropping on AA meetings at the Found Object Wind Chime Museum. The author describes a situation in which a snake bites a dog "on the scrotum." We could tell that Michael had reached that point of the book, because he couldn't contain himself. He clearly had a picture in his mind and wanted to share it all around. While embarrassing and perhaps concerning to some readers, Michael did fill in the gaps left by the author. He could picture the dog screaming, running, and "angry at that snake, so much so that he never wanted to get near a snake again" as Michael put it.

Source: Book cover from *The Boy Who Couldn't Die*, by William Sleator. Copyright © 2005 William Sleator. Reprinted with permission from Harry N. Abrams, Inc.

Of course, not all visualizations are as comical as this. Most visualization occurs as we read and we use them to make meaning, organize our thinking, and monitor our understanding. After all, if you can't visualize what you're reading, you're probably not understanding. Similarly, if you can visualize what you're reading, you're probably going to remember it. Before reading about the dog being bitten by the snake, Michael had read *The Boy Who Couldn't Die* (Sleator, 2004), the story of a rich kid who made a deal with a woman who claims she can make him invincible. The character Ken can't die, but he can kill and does so while he's sleeping. Michael, the reader, is not wealthy; his family qualifies for public assistance. He uses visualizations to fill in the gaps, based on what the author has told him, things he's seen on TV, and his imagination. Our conversations with Michael demonstrate the power of visualizing as he describes what it must feel like for Ken. "Ken felt he didn't have a soul. He was lost and did things he didn't want to do. I saw it all in my mind, you know. Doing things that you're commanded to do, but not knowing why. It's like the movie with the zombies, they didn't have control, either. I pictured Ken walking like that, like the zombies. I also really saw his eyes, you know, with nothing in them, almost dead eyes, but a body moving."

MOVING FROM GOOD TO GREAT

Sometimes we're asked if this is a "natural process"—taking notes, using self-sticking notes, monitoring, reviewing, visualizing, and so on. We think it is. We work with a teacher, Kelly Moore, who regularly reads professional books. If you were to pick any book off of her shelf, you'd find it filled with self-sticking notes. Some of these notes are organizational (e.g., Chapter 3: guided instruction) and others are reactions and thoughts (e.g., which books would be good for this activity?). In addition, Kelly summarizes her thinking about the book and lists questions that she has on paper stuck in the back pages. We don't think she's alone in this. We see real readers taking notes, writing in the margins, and writing on bookmarks all of the time.

Not too long ago, Doug was on the subway in Washington, D.C. Most of the morning commuters were reading. Some were reading novels, others the newspaper. And some were reading informational texts and documents related to their work. Amazingly, almost every reader reading informational texts was reading with a pen or pencil in hand, ready to write. This isn't unusual. In fact, it's often recommended. A simple Google search of "reading with a pen" reveals hundreds of websites devoted to helping people learn from texts. For example, part of the course syllabus for English 1101, Composition and Rhetoric, at Yeshiva University in New York reads:

> You should begin to develop habits common to most careful readers. These include reading things more than once, and reading with a pen(cil) in hand so that you can underline passages that seem important or problematic and can begin to write back questions, comments, and disagreements with the author in the margins.

Great readers are able to monitor what they read, recognizing when they go off track. They apply tools to regain meaning, including rereading, backtracking to pick up the thread of meaning, and using word analysis. This ability to self-monitor becomes largely self-regulated, but requires lots of teacher support to get there. This teacher support comes from teacher modeling to demonstrate how expert readers use this skill, and what they do when they realize the text no longer makes sense.

Great readers also organize as they read, cataloguing and sorting ideas, information, and concepts so that they can be retrieved. This organization of information into more formal schemas cannot be directly observed, so notes serve as a good proxy for witnessing the cognitive organizational strategies utilized by a reader. We want to emphasize that note taking and graphic organizer development should not be done as part of a joyless exercise, but rather because it is necessary for authentic learning. Participation in discussion, journal writing, and oral performance are all examples of authentic purposes for taking notes. As part of this organization, we also encourage students to visualize when the text prompts them to do so. Great readers use visualizing to immerse themselves in a time or place, to more fully understand a process, or to fill in the gaps left by the author. In this way, visualization is an outgrowth of inferencing. Over time, habits of monitoring and organizing help readers to retain what they have read.

Does the student:

Take Notes on Fiction and Nonfiction Texts

- Consider story organization when choosing a graphic organizer?
- Choose the most appropriate organizer to use for a particular purpose?
- Identify important, appropriate information to include on a graphic organizer?
- Understand why and how to use a variety of graphic organizers, for example, story map, Venn diagram, timeline, and so on?
- Recognize the need to go back and check for accuracy and completeness of notes?
- Use completed notes or graphic organizers to support discussion and writing?

Self-Monitor

- Recognize when he or she loses the meaning of the text?
- Reread when something doesn't make sense?
- Distinguish between an important idea and an interesting detail?
- Apply fix-up strategies when meaning is lost?

Visualize

- Use prior knowledge to visualize what is described in a text?
- Use details in a photograph to visualize what an author describes?
- Use details in a text to visualize what an author describes?
- Use sensory information to describe his or her visualization?
- Identify words and phrases that help him or her to visualize?
- Use visualizing in a meaningful way?

Professional Development

1. Invite older siblings (middle school or high school age) to visit the classroom and explain how and why they use note-taking strategies.
2. As adult proficient readers, we sometimes forget how to use self-monitoring strategies because much of the text we read is easy for us. Kill two birds with one stone at a faculty meeting by bringing in a specialized piece of education legislation that's applicable to some students in your school. As everyone reads the piece, ask them to keep track of when their comprehension breaks down, and what strategies they use to fix the confusion.
3. As a faculty, choose a book to read that has been made into a movie. First, read the book, and then watch the movie. Afterwards discuss how scenes in the movie differed from "movies you made in your mind," when you were reading the book. Share this experience with your students.

References

Allington, R. (2002). You can't learn from books you can't read. *Educational Leadership, 60(3)*, 16–19.

Armbruster, B., Anderson, T., & Ostertag, J. (1987). Does text structure/summarization instruction facilitate learning from expository text? *Reading Research Quarterly, 23*, 331–346.

Borduin, B. J., Borduin, C. M., & Manley, C. M. (1994). The use of imagery training to improve reading comprehension of second graders. *Journal of Genetic Psychology, 155*(1), 115–118.

Bromley, K. D. (1999). Key components of sound writing instruction. In L. B. Gambrell, L. M. Morrow, S. B. Neuman, & M. Pressley (Eds.), *Best practices in literacy instruction* (pp. 152–174). New York: Guilford.

Brown, L. K., & Brown, M. (2001). *How to be a friend.* New York: Little Brown and Company.

Burgess, A. (1962). *A clockwork orange.* London: Heinemann.

Burke, J. (2002). *Tools for thought: Graphic organizers for your classroom.* Portsmouth, NH: Heinemann.

Clay, M. M. (2001). *Change over time in children's literacy development.* Portsmouth, NH: Heinemann.

Didion, J. (2005). *The year of magical thinking.* New York: Knopf.

Emery, D. W. (1996). Helping readers comprehend stories from the characters' perspectives. *The Reading Teacher, 49*, 534–541.

Fisher, D., & Frey, N. (2008). *Improving adolescent literacy: Content area strategies at work* (2nd ed.). Upper Saddle River, NJ: Merrill Prentice Hall.

Fleishman, J. (2002). *Phineas Gage: A gruesome but true story about brain science.* Boston: Houghton Mifflin.

Frey, N., & Fisher, D. (2007). *Reading for information in elementary school: Content literacy strategies to build comprehension.* Upper Saddle River, NJ: Merrill Prentice Hall.

Glazer, S. M. (1992). *Reading comprehension: Self-monitoring strategies to develop independent readers.* New York: Scholastic.

Johnson, C. (1955). *Harold and the purple crayon.* New York: HarperTrophy.

Keene, E. O., & Zimmermann, S. (1997). *Mosaic of thought: Teaching comprehension in a reader's workshop.* Portsmouth, NH: Heinemann.

Nelson, P. (2003). *Left for dead: One young man's search for justice for the USS Indianapolis.* New York: Delacorte.

Odorizzi, D. D. (1990). *Georgie the ghost.* New York: Vantage.

Patron, S. (2006). *The higher power of lucky.* New York: Atheneum.

Pauk, W. (1974). *How to study in college.* Boston: Houghton Mifflin.

Pemberton, D. (2005). *The atlas of ancient Egypt.* New York: Harry N. Abrams.

Picoult, J. (2007). *Nineteen minutes.* New York: Atria books.

Pilkey, D. (1997). *The adventures of Captain Underpants.* New York: Blue Sky Press/Scholastic.

Roser, N. L., Martinez, M. G., Yokota, J., & O'Neal, S. (2005). *What a character! Character study as a guide to literary meaning making in grades K–8.* Newark, DE: International Reading Association.

Sleator, W. (2004). *The boy who couldn't die.* New York: Amulet.

Vaughn, S., & Klingner, J. K. (1999). Teaching reading through collaborative strategic reading. *Intervention in School and Clinic, 34*, 284–292.

Ward, H., Andrew, I., & Steer, D. (2004). *Egyptology.* Cambridge, MA: Candlewick.

White, E. B. (1952). *Charlotte's web.* New York: HarperTrophy.

CHAPTER 8

Great Readers Are Critical

Do you find yourself surprised at times when a friend tells you how much he disliked a book that you thought was wonderful? Nancy and Doug disagree on books all the time. Nancy liked the novel *The Book of Salt* (Truong, 2004) and appreciated the author's use of cooking as a metaphor for the protagonist's life. Doug, on the other hand, objected to what he felt was a trivialization of real-life literary and political figures. Doug liked *The Pact: A Love Story* (Picoult, 2006), especially the way the author dealt with the ambiguity of teen suicide. Nancy didn't like the book because she felt the characters and plot did little to inform readers about the complexities of suicide and its aftermath. Both of them count *The Curious Incident of the Dog in the Night-time* (Haddon, 2004) as a favorite, in particular because they felt the author did an excellent job of capturing the voice of a teenage boy with autism.

Being critical is healthy. In the United States being critical is a cornerstone of our democratic government. As citizens, we're allowed to assemble and to share our criticisms without fear of reproach. We are encouraged to notice things that need changing. But being critical does not mean being mean. Often our students need help understanding this distinction. There is a huge difference here. Healthy criticism is constructive and focuses on change and improvement.

As Winston Churchill noted, "Criticism may not be agreeable, but it is necessary. It fulfils the same function as pain in the human body. It calls attention to an unhealthy state of things." And he was right. Criticism creates change. It's about noticing things that need changing. But as Abraham Lincoln wisely suggested, "He has a right to criticize, who has a heart to help." Lincoln's words are worth paying attention to—if we're going to teach students to be critical readers, we must teach them how to learn from the flaws they might see in a text to envision and create something better. Being critical is not an end in itself.

Dating back even further than Churchill or Lincoln, the philosopher Aristotle suggested, "Criticism is something we can avoid easily by saying nothing, doing nothing, and being nothing." Wow, are his words powerful. Aristotle reminds us that we are nothing, living a life not worth living, if we fail to engage in criticism and open ourselves for honest feedback. What a lesson for great readers to understand!

John Graham

WHAT IS CRITICAL LITERACY?

The leading edge of literacy research is critical literacy and the role it plays in comprehension. Critical literacy "views readers as active participants in the reading process and invites them to move beyond passively accepting the text's message to question, examine, or dispute the power relations that exist between readers and authors" (McLaughlin & DeVoogd, 2004, p. 14). The goal of critical literacy is not to criticize a text, but to ask important questions about the author, the characters, and the message. The assumption here is that meaning is jointly constructed by the reader and the text, as opposed to the more passive act of extracting the "right" meaning from the text. This is at the heart of the disagreements about books between Doug and Nancy. We both read the same words, but in some cases had very different viewpoints about the message behind those words, and about the effect the words had on us. Great readers evaluate and question what they read, sometimes disagreeing with the author or one another about the message of the book.

People sometimes confuse the habit of critical literacy and critical thinking. Some teachers have said, "Oh, critical literacy, I do that, it's those inferential and interpretative questions in my textbook." Critical literacy does involve critical thinking skills. When you engage in critical literacy, you go beyond the literal who, what, where, why, and when questions. However, in critical literacy you don't just dig below the surface to see what makes a text work; you also ask, "Is this text working?" and "How is it working?"

Much of our understanding of critical literacy comes to us from our reading colleagues in Australia and New Zealand. The curricula of these countries features a critically literate approach to texts from the earliest grade levels, and students are expected to analyze texts closely for issues of unequal power, author's intent, and alternative perspectives. For example, the Tasmania (Australia) Department of Education reminds teachers that their students should continually ask why a text has been written:

- In whose interest?
- For what purpose?
- Who benefits? (Tasmania Department of Education, 2006, §4)

The overarching goal of critical literacy is to foster astute, sophisticated readers who will query texts for bias of information and omission of other viewpoints. In a digital age in which (sometimes questionable) information has a means of being instantly disseminated and consumed, it is essential for students to be able to read critically, lest they be subjected to misinformation. Perhaps this is why a critical literacy approach is increasingly associated with information and communication technology in schools.

This is not to say that all texts are filled with misinformation, or that all authors have an ulterior motive. Rather, it is a recognition that *no* text is neutral and in fact never can be. All writing is influenced by the author's viewpoints, style, knowledge, and purpose. When we ask our students to "examine the author's craft" or "identify the viewpoint assumed by the author," we are inviting a conversation that bumps up against the edges of critical literacy. These questions prompt our students to think of the authors behind the text. We extend the conversation by encouraging readers to examine the role of power and class, gender and race, and differing perspectives. Figure 8.1 highlights the distinction between critical thinking questions and critical literacy questions.

FIGURE 8.1 Contrasting Critical Thinking and Critical Literacy

Critical Thinking Question	**Critical Literacy Question**
Why did Rosa Parks refuse to move?	Why was Rosa Parks's act of defiance empowering to herself and others? (power)
The family in this book held a big party for their son. How did the son feel about all these presents?	The family in this book held a big party for their son, with lots of presents. Do you think there are other ways a family can celebrate and show their love? (class)
What's similar between a superhero and a president?	Do superheroes do their own laundry? (gender)
What text to self connections did you make to this story?	Do you see yourself represented in this story? (race)
How would you compare the Wicked Witch to Hansel and Gretel?	What story would the Wicked Witch tell about Hansel and Gretel? (alternate perspectives)

Fostering critical literacy analysis occurs primarily through conversation, and the best is often one to one, when the teacher and student can focus carefully on deep understanding. Consider this conversation between Doug and fourth-grader Nayeli about Charlotte, the main character in *Riding Freedom* (Ryan, 1998), the fictionalized account of a girl who disguised herself as a boy in order to make a living as a stagecoach driver in the California goldfields.

Doug: What words would you use to describe Charlie [Charlotte]?
Nayeli: Well, smart, and nice . . . I would say courageous.
Doug: Why courageous?
Nayeli: She did dangerous things . . . like when the bridge collapsed and they fell into the river. But then she worried that the doctor would find out her secret.
Doug: What do you think about that?
Nayeli: I guess I don't know why she didn't just tell people. She was a grown-up, so she didn't have to be a man anymore.
Doug: Why would someone stay a man? Are there reasons why?
Nayeli: Maybe she got used to being a man. Like, she sort of liked the clothes, and everyone calling her Charley.
Doug: Is that OK?
Nayeli: Yeah . . . it's OK. I think her day was easier . . . to be a man. She could go anywhere she wanted.
Doug: Would you want the book to end differently? What if she went back to being Charlotte. Would it be a better ending?
Nayeli: No, I don't think she would be happy. Everyone doesn't have to get married at the end of the story, you know!

In this conversation, Nayeli weighed her perceptions of gender roles against a character who defied the conventions of society. Doug's questions moved from character analysis ("What words would you use to describe Charlie?") to consideration of gender roles and alternative endings of the text. They didn't sit down to have a critical literacy conversation—it was an outgrowth of dialogue between an astute reader and a teacher who encourages students to move beyond the "right answer."

READING THROUGH A CRITICAL LITERACY LENS

In order for critical literacy to become a habit, it needs to be integrated into the discourse of the classroom. It can't be left to occur only during a unit of critical literacy. In critical literacy classrooms, students are routinely asked to evaluate what they are reading in their journals and during conferring. They are encouraged to question traditional roles and messages, and their teachers model alternative perspectives for them.

We are reminded of a conference we had with Tre, a fourth-grade student who was becoming more interested in reading. He was more than halfway through *The Janitor's Boy* (Clements, 2001), the story of Jack, a boy who is ashamed when his friends discover that his father is the school janitor. Jack learns that his father has the keys for the entire school and is pressured by his friends to steal them. Tre told

Source: © 2000 Brian Selznick, is from *The Janitor's Boy*, text by Andrew Clements, cover illustration by Brian Selznick. Used with permission.

us, "It's sad that he treats his dad the way he does, like he's embarrassed. But I can see why he's thinking about those keys. Man, it'd be cool to get in the school at night." We asked him what he thought Jack would do. "I dunno. His pops might lose his job. I think it'll all work out, 'cause a story's 'spposed to have a happy ending." We saw Tre's reference to the ending of story, as an opportunity to engage him in critical literacy, so we asked him if stories *should* have happy endings. By posing this question, we wanted to nudge Tre to question a commonplace element in stories. He answered quickly, "No. Life's not like that. I like it when everything isn't happy, like in Lemony Snicket [books]." We recognized Tre's growth as a great reader in that moment, as he elegantly used summarizing, analyzing, and predicting to discriminate between what stories often do, and what he thought they should do. This represents a move from strategy to habit. His comments also indicated his growth as a critical reader. He acknowledged the traditional storytelling form of the happy ending and challenged the norms of children's literature. Of course, his connection to the Lemony Snicket series also informed us about his development as a reader. Tre is demonstrating a taste for books that are a little edgy, but he still needs the "happy endings" embedded in the "series of unfortunate events"—after all, those unfortunate Baudelaire children keep escaping Count Olaf's clutches, don't they?

Children in the 21st century face a future in which information and misinformation is a keystroke away. To us, the habit of engaging in a critically literate reading is essential. We focus on four elements of critical literacy that we utilize in our classrooms:

1. Question the Commonplace in a Text
2. Consider the Role of the Author
3. Seek Alternative Perspectives
4. Read Critically

Question the Commonplace in a Text

One of the many wonderful things about spending time in the company of children is witnessing their ability to cast a new light on the ordinary. Most of us have had the experience of examining an object we have taken for granted—a leaf, let's say—only to have a child ask a startling question we had never before considered. "Does a leaf feel?" sounds profound coming from a person who isn't old enough to cross the street by herself. The same can be said for the ordinary truths accepted in fiction and nonfiction. Familiar assumptions about the world and its people can retreat from the conscious eye of the reader, like the singular astonishment of a leaf that has long since become part of the background. A critical literacy lens requires that readers seek to disrupt the commonplace through active questioning about topics related to gender, power, class, and race.

One of our favorite techniques to introduce reading with this critical lens is to challenge students to examine the role of heroes and villains in stories. Many young readers are anxious to cast the stories they read as good versus evil, with unflawed champions battling unrepentant scoundrels. Part of this is developmental—a child's world is fairly well demarcated—but it also limits. Writers understand the appeal of a conflicted hero, or a villain with redeeming qualities. We draw our students' attention to the complex characters great writers create and use discussion of these characters to nudge students to a deeper understanding of themselves and the world. *Where the Wild Things Are* (Sendak, 1988) is an enduring classic because Maurice Sendak has delivered such marvelous characters that resonate with readers of all ages. Is Max a bad boy (he chases the dog with a fork and hammers a nail into the wall) or a good one? After all, he is the hero of the book. Can a hero misbehave? And if a hero can misbehave, does that mean we can be naughty and yet still loved?

The examination of heroes and villains extends to more complex texts as well. Of course, the Greek myths are filled with flawed heroes and misunderstood villains. Students can debate whether Pandora was a villain, because she opened the box, or a heroine, because she prevented hope from escaping and thus saved the world. We use the picture book *Pandora* (Burleigh, 2002) with our older students to discuss the theme of hope and condemnation, and make connections to other familiar figures that wreak havoc such as Dr. Seuss's *The Cat in the Hat.* We've been surprised at times with the depth of commentary by middle school students as they comment on the function of scapegoats in societies. For example, sixth-grader Rebecca observed in her journal, "It's easier if you have someone else to blame for your troubles, rather than have to take a look at yourself. People like to say that violent video games cause school shootings, or some kinds of music. But no one seems to want to look at what life might be like for the kids. Maybe there's more to it than just playing some stupid games. It could be more about hurt and anger and hatred."

Questioning Female Gender Roles

The role of Pandora can also be used to challenge assumptions about gender in story. In the traditional myth, Pandora is sent to Prometheus as punishment for stealing the fire Zeus forbade him to take. (Sound familiar?) We ask students to question images in this and other stories of women as an annoyance and draw comparisons to similar modern figures on television (e.g., countless sitcom mothers-in-law).

We use other stories to compare and contrast traditional and nontraditional female gender roles, such as Snow White and *The Paper-Bag Princess* (Munsch, 1988). Princess Elizabeth loses her royal clothing to a dragon's fiery breath and uses a paper bag as a substitute. She rescues a very ungracious Prince Ronald from the dragon's lair, who sniffs that she is sooty and smells like smoke. Munsch's story brilliantly disrupts the commonplace expectations of female gender roles by making Elizabeth the rescuer. Her anger at Ronald is understandable and cheered by readers. We then reread Snow White stories and question why her behavior is so passive. We construct text pairings like this for our older students as well, such as comparing lead characters in *Little Women* (Alcott, 2006) and *Sisterhood of the Traveling Pants* (Brashares, 2001). Both stories describe four very different female characters who are linked by their deep love and respect for one another. However, the historical contexts (the Civil War era versus the present day) allow our students to compare the similarities and differences between society's expectations of young women in relationships.

Questioning Male Gender Roles

Traditional gender roles are confining for boys as well as girls. Robin Mello's (2001) research on perceptions of gender roles in heroes and heroines found that the fourth-grade boys in her study struggled with accepting a hero in a story who could be strong and caring, even as they expressed anxiety about having to give up their own more gentle behaviors when they became men. Stories invite discussion about traditionally assigned gender roles for boys and girls. Some of our favorites for discussion among younger readers on the role of boys in literature include:

- *Oliver Button is a Sissy* (dePaola, 1979)
- *Prince Cinders* (Cole, 1997)
- *Tough Boris* (Fox, 1998)
- *Horace and Boris but Mostly Delores* (Howe, 2003)

Again, our goal in developing a critical literacy habit among our students is not to castigate authors and their works, but to understand where these viewpoints may come from and how they are grounded in the context of the time period and the author's viewpoint, such as Louisa May Alcott's portrayal of young females in *Little Women*, which she wrote in 1868. We also use these texts to help our students know themselves and the world a bit better. Mello (2001) reminds is that "[w]hen students are presented with a variety of gender roles from disparate cultural texts, they begin to examine their own understanding of how to assign value to gender roles and gendered relationships" (p. 554).

Questioning Power and Class

As with gender, power and class issues are easily overlooked by readers unaccustomed to close examination of the commonplace. Students' unquestioned acceptance of power and class can often be found in their own writing. Laurie MacGillivray and Ana Martinez conducted a study that will always remain with us on the writing of second-graders. One girl's story recounted the tale of a princess who wore a plain dress and did not have a ticket to the ball. Her solution was to commit suicide—"death as a solution to unanswered desire" (MacGillivray & Martinez, 1998, p. 54). As teachers, we have seen disconcerting representations of material goods and conformity in our own students' stories—a reminder to us about the pervasiveness of these perceptions.

Fortunately, there are many books that offer ideal opportunities for discussion about social class, social groups, and power. We have used several titles that address various aspects of economic status as a way of representing these issues. We begin by asking our students how they "know" someone is wealthy and we list their predictable responses—a large house, late-model cars, jewelry, and such. We make a similar list about people who have less money and they again offer examples related to possessions. They are sometimes startled when we invite them to describe character traits of the wealthy and poor, but are quickly able to make some fairly subjective remarks regarding intelligence, work ethic, and honesty. We model our thinking using the picture book *Something Beautiful* (Wyeth, 2002), a story of a young girl's search for beauty in a blighted urban neighborhood. Doug begins by writing the word *beautiful* on the whiteboard and asks students to name things that might fit this description. He then shows them the title of the book and begins to read about a similar event in a young girl's classroom. She travels the neighborhood asking people in the community for examples of beauty and learns that a fruit store and the taste of a fried fish sandwich can be beautiful. Doug says, "I can't help but notice that the illustrations show a neighborhood that is not rich. I can tell that's deliberate, and that the author wants us to notice that beauty isn't always something with an expensive price tag."

Nancy uses *A Day's Work* (Bunting, 1997) about a boy and his grandfather looking for day-laborer jobs. Francisco and Abuelo are characters familiar to her students, many of whom have family members who work at similar jobs. Because the young boy is anxious to get paying work for the two of them, he lies about his grandfather's skills, unbeknownst to the older man who he does not speak English. When the job goes badly, Abuelo learns of the deception and refuses payment until the job is done correctly. Nancy and these third-grade students discuss the values that motivate the grandfather, and she asks about the perceptions people hold of day laborers. Raimundo offers that, "Sometimes people treat you like you're going to steal something," and tells the story of his mother's embarrassment at being falsely accused of taking an item from a home she cleaned.

We ask students to read *The Hundred Dresses* (Estes, 2004) to explore the issue of material possessions. In this moving story a girl wears the same dress every day to school, but tells her classmates that she has 100 dresses at home. After discussing the content, we examined other picture books in the classroom and sorted them according to the relative wealth of the main character. Students quickly noticed that most books portrayed a boy or girl living in a suburban, middle-class neighborhood, and those set in an urban center usually had a moderate level of possessions. When characters were identified as being poor, they were most commonly African American or Latino. We ask students to write their reactions to this discovery, and to propose what they could do to change this. Corazon wrote, "We can make a list of books that do a better job of showing that some people have less money" and offered to send this list to the school librarian.

Books such as these have been skillfully written to prompt questioning of the commonplace, so we use them to introduce this habit. However, our goal is for students to apply this habit to wider reading. Therefore, after raising awareness about the portrayal of socioeconomic status, we then invite students to examine other books in the classroom, as well as popular magazines, news reports, and advertisements. By this point, they are more skilled at asking questions about representations of wealth and power.

Consider the Role of the Author

The habit of critical literacy requires that students ask questions not only about the message, but also about the author. As with so many aspects of the habits of great readers, this is an outgrowth of another comprehension strategy—questioning the author (Beck, McKeown, Sandora, Kucan, & Worthy, 1996). You'll recall from Chapter 3 that this approach encourages readers to pose questions one might ask an author if he or she was there in the room ("How did you learn about this topic?" or "Why did you write this book?"). You can see how these questions move readers even closer to asking questions that lead them to evaluate the text. "How did you learn about this topic?" begs another—"Is there other information that you left out of this book?" We think of this as granting young readers permission to *doubt*. What a potent gift. As educators, we want our students to be sophisticated consumers of information.

Our youngest students approach text by actively seeking where the author obtained information. We look for the acknowledgments section in the DK Eyewitness publications because the authors tell us where they get the photographs they use in the books. This strategy also applies to stories. For example, we read the notes from the author in books like *Nana Upstairs and Nana Downstairs* because Tomie dePaola (2000) explains that the story is mostly autobiographical. We consult Steve Jenkins's website (www.stevejenkinsbooks.com) to watch a short film about how he researches and makes accurate collage illustrations of animals for award-winning books like *Actual Size* (2004). We discuss how the author's knowledge of a topic contributes to the quality of the book.

Source: Jacket cover from *The Tequila Worm* by Viola Canales. Used by permission of Wendy Lamb Books, an imprint of Random House Children's Books, a division of Random House, Inc.

Older students are asked to consider the author's motives for writing the book as well. Nancy led a discussion with Trina and Valerie, two seventh-graders who had just finished Viola Canales's *The Tequila Worm* (2005), the story of Sofia, who wins a scholarship to an exclusive boarding school and is confronted with a culture clash of values and mores that differ from her childhood community. Nancy asked the girls why Canales would write this book. Trina immediately mentioned the author's dedication to the teachers and staff of a school with a name similar to the one in the book. "I think she went to boarding school, and she wanted to tell what it was like for her." The girls bandied this idea around for a few minutes, citing examples in the text that would support this conclusion. Nancy then asked them if that meant the book was true. "Oh, no," answered both of them. Valerie continued, "Besides the fact that you can tell it's a novel because the girl's name is different and all, you can't call it true because it's not called an autobiography. If it said that, then it could be true." Nancy reminded them about memoirs as a genre, and these readers began to giggle about "that guy on Oprah" (a reference to disgraced author James Frey). They discussed the controversy about the lack of veracity expected of a memoir, and what an author would need to do in order to make it clear to readers about blending fictionalized accounts with true events. This led Trina to raise the question about the "based on a true story" taglines on so many movies. "How can you know what's true, and what's not?" she asked. "If they tell you to 'write what you know,' how do you know where to draw the line?" Valerie had a reply for her. "I think it's about looking for other info when you read, or when you watch a movie. There's lots of stuff out there about where a story comes from, but you have to know where to go look for it." She went on to describe her efforts to find out to what extent the movie *Pursuit of Happyness* mirrored the memoir of the same name and listed the differences between the two (Gardner, 2006). Nancy wanted to return to the book in hand, so she asked the girls if the author of *The Tequila Worm* would need to omit information. "Well, yeah, sure," answered Valerie. "Like, she can't really write about what the other girls at the boarding school thought of her. She can only describe it the way she sees it."

Identifying the Role Characters Play in Representing the Author's Message

This conversation proved to be the entry point for yet another factor in considering the role of the author. Critical readers understand the agency characters play in representing an author's message. Most commonly, the protagonist serves as the voice of the author and signifies his or her beliefs through dialogue, interior thoughts, and behavior. Nancy asked whether Trina and Valerie thought this was the case in *The Tequila Worm*. Trina mentioned the character Sofia's nightmare about arriving at the dance only to have her schoolmates laugh at her dress that had been transformed into sheets of plastic. "I can see that happening to the author. I know I've had bad dreams like that, too. When it's like all of a sudden there's this horrifying thing happening to you in public and you can't make it stop." Veronica cited Sofia's commitment to writing the traditional stories of the family after the death of her father, and speculated about whether an event like that had occurred in the author's life. "I could see how something like that could change your life," she mused.

Questioning the Author of Informational Texts

Informational texts require examining the role of the author, too, and there is perhaps no more important place to do so than on the Internet. When readers apply critical reading strategies to this genre, they ask questions that examine the sources of information the author used to write the text and the role of the author in developing the text. They also consider the purpose for the text and how the author might have obtained the information. The informational texts that our students encounter on the Internet often require that our students develop their critical lens. For example, here's how we used conversation to nudge Jon, an eighth-grader, to think critically about the information he was reading on the Internet.

Jon is a dedicated fan of skateboarding and has been interested in learning more about *parkour*, an aggressive form of athleticism that turns urban landscapes into obstacle courses. Participants use movements influenced by martial arts, gymnastics, and combat training. Jon consulted Wikipedia for some basic information and learned about the philosophical falling out between the founders of the discipline. Jon's knowledge of this controversy led him to consider his own views of the activity—is it a competitive sport or an art form? We asked him about his own opinions and discussed the rhetoric he was likely to encounter on the websites. Jon described for us the kind of boastful talk he hears and uses when skateboarding with others (he referred to it as "dissin") and predicted that some sites might contain language or information that would be insulting or untrue. He then read several websites from both points of view and concluded that he was more interested in the technical execution of the moves, rather than in competition. He therefore decided to spend his time exploring a website associated with founder David Belle. He has learned how to execute a few basic moves such as wall pops, rolls, and vaults, and is currently perfecting his cat jump. He participates in an online community of *parkour* enthusiasts in the San Diego area. There's not much available to Jon on *parkour* in traditional print genre, so his application of critical literacy helps him to navigate digital information.

Great readers who are in the habit of considering the role of the author don't always need to locate the "right" answer, or even seek it out. Rather, readers like Trina and Valerie demonstrate that they are conscious of the hand of the author in the works they read and are comfortable with contemplating his or her influence. Jon's analysis of the various *parkour* websites he visited began with a quick look at the source. Jon had developed the habit of questioning the role of the author in order to understand and evaluate the information. This not only deepens their understanding of what they read, but it also gives them insight into their own writing lives.

Seek Alternative Perspectives

The signature of a critical reader is the ability to actively consider alternative perspectives to the one presented in the text. As a reminder, the emphasis is not on a default position that all authors have actively sought to obscure any other perspectives, rather that every writer adopts a particular lens, and that there may be other viewpoints worth considering as well. In particular, historical and cultural considerations can influence the message of the text. This is not an understanding typically assumed by most young readers. Sam Wineburg, the noted historian and educator, found that historians and students differ in the reading of documents in one crucial way—the students did not take into account who wrote it or when it was written. Instead, these "novice historians" took the information at face value and did not understand the implications of authorship and place on writing (1991). He calls this a difference in "epistemological stance" (p. 495); we would attribute it to "uncritical literacy." Either way, this is a troubling finding, especially when one considers the implications. For example, we don't want readers to accept a tree logging company's perspective without also hearing from a botanist (or vice versa). It isn't hyperbole to assert that the ability to seek out multiple perspectives in order to make decisions and take action is at the heart of our democratic process.

Now of course, the ways we model multiple perspectives aren't always so serious, especially with young readers. Our intent is to foster the habit of considering more than one perspective. Primary teachers everywhere use *The True Story of the Three Little Pigs* (Scieszka, 1999) to encourage students to reconsider the traditional fairy tale. The wolf's explanation that "the real story is about a sneeze and a cup of sugar" (p. 6) is slyly humorous and invites readers to notice when the wolf seems to "protest too much," as the Bard would say. We also like *The Three Little Wolves and the Big Bad Pig* (Trivizas, 1997), *The Wolf Who Cried Boy* (Hartman, 2004), as well as Alvin Grawowsky's *Another Point of View* series that features both sides of familiar tales.

The habit of considering multiple viewpoints doesn't necessarily come easily to older readers, either. Doug sometimes models shifting views with one of his favorite picture books, *The Other Side* (Woodson, 2001), with its beautiful watercolor illustrations of two children, one Caucasian and the other African American, who have a fence that keeps them apart. Doug thinks aloud to his students about the author's use of the fence as a metaphor for the cultural and racial divide of the time and notes the visual shifts in perspectives mirrored by the artist. He extends their understanding of multiple viewpoints by introducing the poem "Honeybees" from Paul Fleischman's award-winning book *Joyful Noise: Poems for Two Voices* (2004). The verse starkly represents the two very different life experiences of the queen bee ("I'm loved and I'm lauded/I'm outranked by none") and a drone ("Then I pack combs with pollen/Not my idea of fun") as they simultaneously share their positions (pp. 30–31). Nancy counts *Voices in the Park* (Browne, 2001) as a favorite for modeling the same concepts. The author identifies four voices (two children and their parents), each denoted by a different typeface. An unemployed father and his playful daughter meet a wealthy mother and her morose son in a park and describe four different viewpoints of the encounter. Issues of class and power are played out across the pages of this deceptively complex picture book.

Of course, the study of history itself is in exploring the many viewpoints of those who witnessed important events. *We Were There, Too! Young People in U.S. History* (Hoose, 2001) has proven to be an indispensable information source for learning more about eyewitnesses to history. This book is filled with the accounts of children and adolescents who were present at key points in our country's history, including a resident of Jamestown in the 1600s, a Chinese immigrant in 1850s San Francisco, and an African American student who faced a mob in Little Rock in 1957. Children are rarely mentioned in history books, and we find that our students appreciate learning about the experiences of young participants. Another recommendation is *Crossing the Delaware: A History in Many Voices* (Peacock, 1998). This book mixes informational text about Washington's crossing at Trenton with primary source documents and fictional letters from soldiers on both sides of the river. The author continues with this theme in *At Ellis Island: A History in Many Voices* (Peacock, 2007), adopting both contemporary and historical points of view about this gateway for so many of America's immigrants.

We count ourselves among the many Jane Yolen fans for her fine books that invite readers to consider multiple perspectives. One of our favorites is *Encounter* (Yolen, 1992), written for the 500th anniversary of Columbus's landing on San Salvador. The illustrations by David Shannon mirror the accompanying text as they visualize the events through the eyes of a young Taino boy. We have introduced this text by asking a fellow teacher to enter our classroom while we are at lunch in order to remove conspicuous items like charts and easels. Our students notice the missing objects right away when they return and begin to speculate on what might have occurred. Our conspirator then returns to say that she has "discovered" these items and has taken them back to her classroom. We allow our students to articulate why this is unfair and begin to list their arguments on the board. After returning the purloined items, we connect this to the clashing perspectives of European explorers and indigenous people the world over about the concept of "discovery." Yolen's book sensitively represents this viewpoint and serves as an excellent springboard for student research. We also read books from the explorer's perspective, including Peter Sis's *Follow the Dream: Christopher Columbus* (2003). As critically literate readers, we want our students to be able to formulate informed opinions and to recognize the complexities of human history. We deliberately choose complex topics like this so that students can wrestle with issues that defy easy explanations and authentically seek to educate themselves about a topic.

Read Critically

"Wait a minute," you're thinking. "I thought this whole chapter was about reading critically! How is this different from the other habits you just told me about?" A fair question (and a sign you've been monitoring as you read). So far, we've discussed consciously adopting a habit of questioning the traditions, the author's message, and the viewpoints in a reading. But we haven't yet discussed the role that bias can play, or how one ultimately goes about evaluating what's been read. Perhaps a better way to describe it is to say that we want our students to recognize "spin" when they see it. We turn to Brooks Jackson and Kathleen Hall Jamieson from the Annenberg Institute for a definition:

> "Spin" is a polite word for deception. Spinners mislead by means that range from subtle omissions to outright lies. Spin paints a false picture of reality by bending the facts, mischaracterizing the words of others, ignoring or denying crucial evidence, or just "spinning a yarn"—by making things up. (2007, p. vii)

Reading critically ultimately means being able to transform information (and misinformation) using a healthy sense of doubt. As adult readers, our ability to deploy our "doubt shields" has been finely developed over the years. We read more skeptically when we receive an e-mail promising easy riches in a bank account on another continent, or when we peruse the grocery store checkout headlines about alien babies and bees that make mayonnaise. We *hrumph* at the ads in the back of the magazine that promise we'll lose weight while we sleep. But how did you learn to do this? Hopefully, it wasn't all through personal trial and error (although Nancy can remember being bitterly disappointed by the Sea Monkeys she bought as a child, none of whom seemed to be wearing little crowns). Chances are good that as you expanded your sources you began to compare, analyze, and evaluate. All these years later, you are not about to be suckered into buying that new overnight face cream just because it boasts that it will eliminate 27% of fine lines after two weeks of continuous use!

We've made light of serious topic, but in truth there's nothing more important than equipping our students with the ability to discriminate between good sense and nonsense. They are vulnerable to the sway of appealing but deceptive information, especially in a digital age when sources are increasingly hard to check. Advertisements are increasingly sophisticated and range from product placements in movies to psychologically exploitative marketing that makes toddlers feel inferior if they don't have the latest widget.

Those very advertisements are a great starting point for fostering discussion about media messages. Ask students to analyze cereal boxes during a nutrition unit, or compare print ads for sneakers that run the price gamut. During one such lesson, fourth-grader Jeremy pointed out that the priciest shoes included a photograph of an athlete, while the inexpensive ones offered a shot of the shoe only, with no human image. "It's like it doesn't even matter to have people [in the ad]," he commented. "Maybe it costs too much." That is a young consumer's very astute observation.

Word choice is a factor in detecting bias as well. Headlines are an excellent tool for focusing on the use of loaded terminology. Doug's students work together in pairs to locate words that represent positive and negative terms for similar concepts. For example, seventh-grade readers Alycia and Graham cut out the following words in headlines from one daily paper.

- Police, cop, officers, law enforcement
- Soldiers, militants, rebels, guerillas, insurgents, military, army, combatants
- Politicians, lawmakers, elected officials, senator, pols, legislator, politicos
- Victim, criminal, alleged bandit, casualty
- Explain, demands, justifies, commands, asks, claimed

They debated the relative positive and negative connotations of their words and glued them onto paint chip cards donated from the local hardware store for an activity called shades of meaning (Frey & Fisher, 2006). They arranged the words on a continuum using the deepening shades of paint to represent the increasing degrees of intensity associated with the word. They finished by writing a series of sentences that varied by only one word.

- School board member *asks about* budget decisions.
- School board member *explains* budget decisions.
- School board member *demands* budget decisions.
- School board member *justifies* budget decisions.
- School board member *claims* budget decisions.
- School board member *commands* budget decisions.

They discussed the subtle implications of altering one word and noticed that the undertone shifts from query to domination. Alycia and Graham's close reading of their sentences invites them to notice what Francine Prose calls "the crucial revelations . . . in the spaces *between* words" (2007, p. 19).

Sometimes recognition of the influence of bias requires this parsing of sentences at the word level. At other times, it is an evaluation of the author's voice. Readers are familiar with the unreliable narrator in fiction—one who manipulates the truth, withholding crucial details that would otherwise illuminate. The

John Graham

unnamed narrator of the Lemony Snicket series is an example of this rhetorical device. An astute reader notices that the narrator signals his undependability early in the first book: "I don't know if you've noticed this, but first impressions are often entirely wrong" (Snicket, 1999, p. 27). Younger readers can find examples of this in *Cat in the Hat* books, and in *Dear Mr. Blueberry* (James, 1996) as we witness the contrast between the letters exchanged by a girl and her teacher concerning a large whale in her backyard pond. In these cases, the unreliable narrator is used for comic effect, but in informational texts, this is harder to discern, particularly because the writer is so unlikely to reveal his or her bias. Letters are useful for discovering the author's bias. The letters to the editor in the local newspaper are an ongoing source of material for such analysis. After all, does our opinion change when we notice that a letter minimizing the environmental impact of gas-guzzling SUVs comes from the owner of an auto dealership selling these vehicles? Political cartoons, propaganda, and slanted media coverage serve as rich materials for such explanations. The searchable WebQuest database at San Diego State University provides students with materials for examination of bias (www.webquest.sdsu.edu).

Besides word choice and author bias, a final consideration to reading critically is to consider the veracity of the content itself. Nancy models the application of content analysis by examining advertising posters from the Museum of Questionable Medical Devices at the Science Museum of Minnesota. Advertisements touting hair removal with X-rays, psychographs that analyzed character traits based on the bumps on a skull, and radioactive tonic waters are just a few of the marvels collected and displayed. (A caution to teachers: Some of the devices on this website are not suitable for classroom use. Be sure to choose in advance which posters you will use.) She follows this with readings from *The Head Bone's Connected to the Neck Bone: The Weird, Wacky, and Wonderful X-ray* (McClafferty, 2001) and *Something Out of Nothing: Marie Curie and Radium* (McClafferty, 2006) to compare information about radiation against the spurious claims of disreputable advertisers.

There are, of course, dozens of examples of ways to teach the habit of reading critically. The commonality, however, is in presenting students with sources of valid information for them to use to compare against suspected propaganda. Because critical reading is ultimately predicated on an assumption of an informed reader, the habit of reading critically is developed through a consistent disposition to approach information with a degree of skepticism and to confirm or disconfirm the reliability by seeking out other sources of information. That spirit of inquiry is necessary to feed an informed mind. As Carl Sagan offered, "Skeptical scrutiny is the means . . . by which deep thoughts can be winnowed from deep nonsense."

MOVING FROM GOOD TO GREAT

The ability to read with a critical eye is arguably the capstone habit of a great reader because it requires the consolidation of all the skills and strategies taught to readers. Therefore, moving from good to great means showing students how you marshal all the skills and strategies at your disposal as you read critically. Model your own thinking as you question, monitor, analyze, and evaluate. Show them that great readers are *consumers* of text, in every sense of the word. They read widely and see themselves as readers, consuming voluminous amounts of written words each day. They are also consumers in the market sense—they are the audience that must be satisfied with the information presented to them.

Jackson and Jamieson (2007) offer nine rules for being critical consumers of information, and they are an apt summary for critical literacy.

1. You can't be *completely* certain.
2. You *can* be certain enough.
3. Look for general agreement among experts.
4. Check primary sources.
5. Know what counts.
6. Know who's talking.
7. Seeing shouldn't necessarily be believing.
8. Cross-check everything that matters.
9. Be skeptical, but not cynical.

In an age when information and misinformation appears before our learners at lightning speed, the habit of critical reading will determine their own future freedoms.

Does the student:

Question the Commonplace in a Text

- Identify heroes and villains in a story and tell how the behavior of those characters varies from archetypal behavior?
- Identify the roles of men and women in a story and recognize how those roles differ from what might be expected?
- Identify ways in which characters in a story treat other characters based on gender stereotypes?
- Identify the status of characters and recognize how status affects a character's power and how the character is treated by others?

Consider the Role of the Author

- Identify possible sources of information that an author uses to write a story or nonfiction text?
- Identify material that might be factual in a piece of fiction?
- Recognize the possible motives that an author might have for writing?
- Explain how characters represent the author's message?

Seek Alternative Perspectives

- Understand the term *perspective?*
- Identify the perspectives of different characters in a text?
- Retell a story from another character's perspective?
- Explain the historical or cultural influences on a book?
- Compare and contrast alternative perspectives between texts?

Read Critically

- Recognize bias demonstrated by a person in a book or by the author of a text?
- Recognize where bias is harmful to others?
- Identify gaps in information in a text and explain how to learn more?
- Form and support value judgments, or opinions, about what he or she reads?

Professional Development

1. It's hard for us to teach critical literacy, if we haven't had critical conversations about books. If the concepts in this chapter are new to you, form a study group at school that specifically examines books from a critical stance.
2. Invite students to create a critical literacy handbook for your school that focuses on the Internet.
3. Student literature discussion groups or book clubs are great places to introduce critical literacy. However, as pointed out in this chapter, students and teachers need practice in raising the level of conversation to a critical stance. Tape several discussion groups at different grade levels, and bring them to a grade-level or faculty meeting. Together, brainstorm questions or prompts that would deepen the discussion.

References

Alcott, L. M. (2006). *Little women.* Fairfield, IA: First World Library.

Beck, I. L., McKeown, M. G., Sandora, C., Kucan, L., & Worthy, J. (1996). Questioning the author. *The Elementary School Journal, 95*, 395–414.

Brashares, A. (2001). *Sisterhood of the traveling pants.* New York: Delacorte.

Browne, A. (2001). *Voices in the park.* New York: DK Publishing.

Bunting, E. (1997). *A day's work.* New York: Clarion.

Burleigh, R. (2002). *Pandora.* Silver Whistle.

Canales, V. (2005). *The tequila worm.* New York: Random House.

Clements, A. (2001). *The janitor's boy.* New York: Aladdin.

Cole, B. (1997). *Prince Cinders.* New York: Putnam.

DePaola, T. (1979). *Oliver Button is a sissy.* San Diego: Harcourt Brace.

DePaola, T. (2000). *Nana upstairs and Nana downstairs.* New York: Putnam.

Estes, E. (2004). *The hundred dresses.* New York: Harcourt.

Fleischman, P. (2004). *Joyful noise: Poems for two voices.* New York: HarperTrophy.

Fox, M. (1998). *Tough Boris.* New York: Voyager.

Frey, N., & Fisher, D. (2006). *Reading for information in elementary school: Content literacy strategies to build comprehension.* Upper Saddle River, NJ: Pearson Merrill Prentice Hall.

Gardner, C. (2006). *The pursuit of happyness.* New York: Amistad.

Grawowsky, A. (1994). *Cinderella/that awful Cinderella: A classic tale.* Orlando, FL: Steck-Vaughn.

Haddon, M. (2004). *The curious incident of the dog in the night-time.* New York: Vintage.

Hartman, B. (2004). *The wolf who cried boy.* New York: Puffin.

Hoose, P. (2001). *We were there, too! Young people in U.S. history.* New York: Farrar, Straus, and Giroux.

Howe, J. (2003). *Horace and Boris but mostly Delores.* New York: Aladdin.

Jackson, B., & Jamieson, K. H. (2007). *UnSpun: Finding facts in a world of disinformation.* New York: Random House.

James, S. (1996). *Dear Mr. Blueberry.* New York: Aladdin.

Jenkins, S. (2004). *Actual size.* New York: Houghton Mifflin.

MacGillivray, L., & Martinez, A. M. (1998). Princesses who commit suicide: Primary children writing within and against gender stereotyping. *Journal of Literacy Research, 30*, 53–84.

McClafferty, C. K. (2001). *The head bone's connected to the neck bone: The weird, wacky, and wonderful x-ray.* New York: Farrar, Straus, and Giroux.

McClafferty, C. K. (2006). *Something out of nothing: Marie Curie and radium.* New York: Farrar, Straus, and Giroux.

McLaughlin, M., & DeVoogd, G. L. (2004). *Critical literacy: Enhancing students' comprehension of text.* New York: Scholastic.

Mello, R. (2001). Cinderella meets Ulysses. *Language Arts, 78*, 548–555.

Munsch, R. (1988). *The paper-bag princess.* Toronto, Canada: Ammick.

Peacock, L. (1998). *Crossing the Delaware: A history in many voices.* New York: Atheneum.

Peacock, L. (2007). *At Ellis Island: A history in many voices.* New York: Atheneum.

Picoult, J. (2006). *The pact: A love story.* New York: Harper Perennial.

Prose, F. (2007). *Reading like a writer: A guide for people who love books and for those who want to write them.* New York: Harper Perennial.

Ryan, P. M. (1998). *Riding freedom.* New York: Scholastic.

Scieszka, J. (1999). *The true story of the three little pigs.* New York: Viking.

Sendak, M. (1988). *Where the wild things are.* HarperCollins.

Sis, P. (2003). *Follow the dream: Christopher Columbus.* New York: Knopf.

Snicket, L. (1999). *The bad beginning: A series of unfortunate events, book 1.* New York; HarperCollins.

Tasmania Department of Education. (2006). *English learning area: Critical literacy.* Retrieved May 31, 2007 from http://wwwfp.education.tas.gov.au/English/critlit.htm

Trivizas, E. (1997). *The three little wolves and the big bad pig.* New York: Aladdin.

Truong, M. (2004). *The book of salt.* New York: Vintage.

Wineburg, S. S. (1991). On the reading of historical texts: Notes on the breach between school and academy. *American Education Research Journal, 28*, 495–519.
Woodson, J. (2001). *The other side.* New York: Putnam.
Wyeth, S. D. (2002). *Something beautiful.* New York: Dragonfly.
Yolen, J. (1992). *Encounter.* San Diego: Harcourt Brace Jovanovich.

INDEX

C

H